Asian Cooking Made Simple

A CULINARY JOURNEY ALONG THE SILK ROAD AND BEYOND

by Habeeb Salloum

Acknowledgments

I wish to thank my two daughters, Muna Salloum and Leila Salloum Elias, for their valuable advice and help in testing and tasting a number of the dishes. As well, I would like to thank them for proofreading the completed manuscript. They have through the years been not only loving daughters but also working colleagues and advisors.

In addition, I wish to thank all those authors whose books I studied to gain a better knowledge of the foods of the Asian countries. Further, I wish to thank all my colleagues and friends for their valuable advice in preparing and tasting the recipes.

Finally, I wish to thank Eric P. Hanson, who took on the task of designing this cookbook to bring out the beauty of Asian cuisine. Moreover, I wish to express my deepest gratitude to Kathy Springmeyer, Director of Publications at Sweetgrass Books, whose patience, diligence, and advice made this project a wonderful experience.

ISBN 10: 1-59152-134-3
ISBN 13: 978-1-59152-134-1

Published by Habeeb Salloum

© 2014 by Habeeb Salloum

All photography and food styling by Muna Salloum

You may order extra copies of this book by calling Farcountry Press toll free at (800) 821-3874.

sweetgrassbooks
a division of Farcountry Press

Produced by Sweetgrass Books.
PO Box 5630, Helena, MT 59604; (800) 821-3874; www.sweetgrassbooks.com.

Printed in China.

18 17 16 15 14   1 2 3 4 5

Table of Contents

The Asian Kitchen…..5
Why a Simplified Asian Cookbook?…..9
Asian Condiments…..11

The Asian Kitchen

Thoughts of Asian cuisine usually evoke the foods from India to China and Southeast Asia. Yet, Asian food is much more. One must not forget the foods of the Middle East and Central Asia. Asian lands stretch from the European borders of Turkey and the Syrian coastline in the west to the Philippines in the east; from Siberia in the north to Sri Lanka and the southern Arabian Peninsula in the south.

It would not be far-fetched to say that much of the world's foods had their origin in this vast area of the world, which is inhabited by some two-thirds of humankind. In these countries where civilizations sprung, a wide-ranging cuisine has evolved through the centuries. This culinary world is a banquet of delights, featuring the fantastic gastronomic arts of lands such as China, India, and the Middle East.

There is enormous variation in the kitchens of the Asian countries, ranging from the spicy foods of Southeast Asia to the tactfully spiced dishes in Japan. Except for some parts of northern China, rice is a staple throughout. In addition, you'll find many types of breads, usually from wheat. Dairy products and meat dominate the kitchens of Central Asia and the lands spreading northward from northern China, India, Pakistan, and westward to the Mediterranean. The daily menus are quite different from those in East Asia, where rice and vegetables are the main foods, with only a little meat.

Asian cuisine in the Western world has numerous connotations. At times it is a term only associated with the foods of the Indian subcontinent, East Asia, and Southeast Asia. Only rarely does it include the cuisine of the Polynesian islands or the culinary arts of Central and West Asia or those of the Middle East.

Food historians have often divided Asian cuisine into three main regions. The first area is Southeast Asia, which includes Thailand, Laos, Cambodia, Vietnam, Indonesia, Malaysia, Singapore, Brunei, and the Philippines. This region features lightly prepared spicy and aromatic foods, using herbs such as basil, cilantro, lemongrass, and mint, and quickly stir-fried. The second area is China and Korea, emphasizing fats, oils, and sauces. The third region includes India, Pakistan, Sri Lanka, and Burma, which have been influenced greatly by Persian and Arab foods such as wheat, bread, milk, and meat. Western Asia, which includes the Middle East, is often not considered a part of Asia despite the solid trade and other human connections between western and eastern Asia since the earliest of times. The Silk Road that connected China with the Syrian coastline; the Arab traders who, even before Roman times, carried the goods of the Far East back to Arab lands, Europe, and beyond; and the Muslim religion, which spread to the heart of China, all had a hand in the intermixing of culinary arts.

The basic cuisine of East Asia is the Chinese kitchen, the best known of all Asian styles of cooking. It is without question one of the richest and most diverse kitchens in the world, consisting of thousands of dishes. Basically, it includes northern and southern styles. The southern dishes emphasize freshness and tenderness; northern dishes are known for their use of oil, vinegar, and garlic. There are many styles included in these foods, such as Anhui, Beijing, Cantonese, Fujian, Guangdong, Hunan, Jiangsu, Shandong, Shanghai, Szechuan, Xi'an, Zhejiang, and the cuisines of minorities such as Hui, Mongolian, Uyghur, and Tibetan. China has a highly sophisticated food culture, its fascination with food rooted in the country's 5,000 years of culinary history. Because of this food culture, Chinese food has developed into a gourmet heaven and gained a high reputation throughout the globe for its many enticing features, including appearance, daintiness, smell, taste, and texture. Such is the importance of food that a popular greeting among the people is, "Have you eaten already?"

Through the centuries, Chinese culinary traditions have evolved and been perfected—they have withstood the test of time. Many of the modern Chinese dishes were created under the Imperial Ming Dynasty (A.D. 1368–1644). The following dynasty, the Manchu (1644–1911), created an era of peace and prosperity that further developed the cuisine. This is what we, today, call authentic Chinese cuisine. There is no doubt that the thousands of years of experimentation with nature's bounty are the basis of the rich and vibrant culinary heritage of China.

Chinese cuisine has had a great influence on the cuisines of neighboring lands—a spillover from which the dishes of adjoining countries were developed according to their special circumstances. As a result of Islam's entrance into China under the Mongols, Chinese cuisine in the north and west differs somewhat from that of the rest of China. Lamb and mutton and generally dishes without pork are features of these regions. As a result, the foods in those parts of China today differ from those in the south, in this case, because of non-Chinese influences.

It was a similar story in the surrounding countries. Japanese cuisine emphasizes deep-frying of meats and vegetables due to the Portuguese who once controlled a part of the country. In the former French colonies of Cambodia, Laos, and Vietnam, many dishes carry the French imprints. Malaysia and Singapore were British colonies, and British influences run their kitchens. In the same fashion, the Dutch who ruled most of Indonesia for some 300 years left their mark in the culinary habits of that country. As well, the Philippines, once ruled by the Spanish and then the Americans, inherited those food legacies. Farther west, it was the same story, where Western colonialists influenced cuisine in the Indian subcontinent and the Middle East.

Next to China, the vast and ancient Indian subcontinent has a wide-ranging cuisine that is regarded as being among the world's greatest. The subcontinent includes the kitchens of India, Bangladesh, Pakistan, Sri Lanka, Nepal, and Bhutan, whose cuisines are dominated by rice and curry dishes.

The foods of these lands have traditions stretching back some 3,000 years. Their kitchens offer abundant culinary masterpieces as diverse as the peoples and their history. The essence of these cuisines lies in the variety of spices available to the cook, which contributes greatly to the gastronomy of these countries.

Traditional and regional specialties abound in India. Curries from Chettinadu, Portuguese-influenced foods from Goa, tropical fruits and seafood from Kerala, delicious kebabs and biryanis of Lucknow, tandoori *delights from the Punjab,* and exotic and spicy dishes from Tamil Nadu, are a few of the specialties that make India a continent of seductive flavors.

Throughout Asia are some common foods, as well as others that have nothing in common. Rice is the staff of life in Northeast and Southeast Asia but becomes less important as one moves westward through Central Asia, the Indian subcontinent, and the Middle East.

Of all the great cuisines in the world, the Arab and Iranian kitchens are, perhaps, the least known in the West. Stretching from the borders of the Indian subcontinent to the Mediterranean Sea, the Arab/Iranian lands form an entire region of diverse culinary delights. This virtually unknown cookery has a fascinating and colorful history. In the seventh century, the Arabs from the Arabian Peninsula who arrived on the shores of the eastern Mediterranean Sea found a wide variety of foods, some of which went back to the beginning of civilized history. From these newly occupied lands—the cradle of civilizations that had risen, flourished, and declined—they inherited a rich cuisine. Sumerian, Babylonian, Phoenician, Hittite, Aramaen, Assyrian, Egyptian, Nabatean, Greek, Byzantine, Roman, and especially Persian, were some of the bygone empires that contributed to the Arabs' newly established kitchen.

The simple dishes they had brought with them from the Arabian Peninsula were added to the accumulation of edibles they found among the conquered peoples. Later, the Turks, and after them the European colonialists, added to this repertoire of foods. Further, the many exotic minorities that inhabited the Arab world, such as the Armenians, Berbers, and Kurds, contributed their own peculiarities, as did the religious communities such as the Copts, Druze, Maronites, and Sephardim Jews. All of these influences, no matter how acquired, were enhanced and developed to produce the incredibly rich modern Arab and Iranian cuisines.

As one moves westward from the Indian subcontinent, rice is supplemented with a variety of leavened and unleavened breads and other wheat products such as farina and bulgur. Somewhat of an enigma are the pasta products, such as spaghetti and noodles, thought by many to have been brought back to Italy from China by Marco Polo, somewhat going against the theory that wheat products become more and more important as one travels in Asia toward the setting sun. The Marco Polo story could, however, be totally incorrect. Food historians have found evidence in the last century that pasta was first made in the Middle East and carried eastward and westward by traders. Indeed, the first people historically to have used a form of pasta were said to be the Babylonians. In China, noodles made from rice, eggs, or potatoes are found more often than those made of wheat.

There are a number of much-used herbs common to all of Asia: basil, cilantro, and mint flourish almost everywhere in the tropical and subtropical areas of the continent. Of course, there are many varieties of these herbs, such as Thai basil's purple stems and licorice flavor, which are uniquely different from most other basil.

As for spices, Asia is the continent whence most of the spices of the world originate and where they are the basis of the tasty foods of that part of the world. Aniseed, cardamom, cinnamon, cloves, coriander, cumin, ginger, mace, nutmeg, saffron, sumac, turmeric, and others all are employed in the Asian kitchens to produce appetizing, enhanced tastes. In the Middle Ages, wars were fought, empires rose and fell, and sailing voyages explored the globe searching for these spices. Today, they are found in kitchens around the world—much different from the Middle Ages when, in Europe, an ounce of cloves, nutmeg, or pepper was worth an ounce of gold.

The two most important food enhancers in all of Asia are garlic and ginger, common across the huge continent. Every homemaker and chef in Asia uses garlic. The use of ginger, however, becomes rare as one travels westward to the Middle East. In all probability, both became known in China at almost the same time that rice began to be cultivated.

Chiles are very common in Southwest and Southeast Asia, but become rare as one moves to the Middle Eastern countries edging the Mediterranean. Strangely, chile peppers are not native to Asia. All types of peppers originated in the Americas and were brought to the region by European conquerors, explorers, and traders. These peppers, especially the hot varieties that today are so essential in Asian cooking, arrived in the sixteenth century, and by the seventeenth century were being widely used. Other spices and herbs were used to create hot dishes before the introduction of these peppers from the Americas.

Curry sauces are found mostly in the Indian subcontinent. To the southeast they are, as a rule, based on coconut milk; to the southwest, curries are generally based on yogurt. Curry sauces are found in parts of China and, to some extent, in Southeast Asia. The creation of curry sauces is an Indian invention that spread east, where the people modified the original by substituting coconut milk for yogurt as the basis for the sauce.

In Chinese cuisine, soy sauce is the king of condiments. While countries south of China use soy sauce, fish sauce is the overwhelming favorite. Soy sauce disappears from the menu as one travels westward and beyond. Yet, the Romans had a concoction, called garum, that was similar to fish sauce, and the medieval Arabs had a fermented liquid sauce called muri, made from barley, though both today are lost to the vestiges of time.

Another food enhancer much employed in cooking, especially in Southeast Asia, is lime, native to Indonesia and Malaysia. In addition to its juice, cooks often use the leaves of the lime tree, and pulp, and zest of the lime tree. In the same region are another two condiments: lemongrass and galangal make the cuisines of the region unique. There are numerous other flavoring agents in other parts of Asia, such as pomegranate syrup, fenugreek sauces, and za'tar—a mixture of sumac, ground roasted chickpeas, sesame seeds, and thyme—adding to the enticement of Asian cuisine's fragrance and heavenly flavors.

For fats, ghee and clarified butter are favored in the Indian subcontinent and westward. Olive oil, mostly pressed in modern factories, takes over as one nears the Mediterranean coastline. Vegetable oils such as peanut, sesame, and sunflower are overwhelmingly used in China and the other countries in the Far East.

Cooking and utensils vary throughout Asia. In China, a type of frying pan called the wok is the basic cooking utensil. China's stir-fry technique using vegetable oils and quick frying produces dishes that look fresh, colorful, and appetizing. The tanour, a type of oven found in the Indian subcontinent and westward, has been used to bake bread and other foods for thousands of years. For anyone who enjoys the taste of freshly baked bread, there is no better treat than to munch on hot baked bread just out of the tanour.

In this extensive and fantastic world of cookery, no one can possibly give a comprehensive overview of all the foods. However, a sampling of this colossal Asian kitchen will give the reader entering this culinary world a taste of countless foods, some as old as time. For gourmet travelers, it is a journey of the taste buds that makes life worth living.

Why a Simplified Asian Cookbook?

"It's so delicious! I love Chinese food!" my daughter remarked as she feasted on juicy seafood cooked Chinese-style. "Soon you will be cooking these dishes yourself," I answered. "I'm working at simplifying a series of Asian dishes." I smiled as I dug in to help her finish the platter of mouthwatering seafood.

The foods of China have been among my favorites from the time I was a young boy and was introduced into the culinary world of that ancient land. China, which gave the world gunpowder, paper, paper currency, silk, and much more, has in the last century succeeded in continuing these contributions by spreading its cuisine to the four corners of the globe. Hence, when I began to think of simplifying Asian food recipes, China was on my mind. I found that there are no magic formulas to cook Asian dishes. Having access to special utensils and cooking tools and ingredients is no problem in our evolving world. In the large urban centers in the West, anyone who wishes to cook Asian dishes should encounter no problems in finding the herbs, spices, and other ingredients. The only drawback for people who are not familiar with Asian food is the complicated-looking recipes. Therefore, my cookbook! I have traveled in many of the Asian countries, tasted their foods in the homes of friends and colleagues, and talked about these foods with immigrants from these lands. In the process, it occurred to me that since I have been creating and writing about food for years, why not simplify the Asian dishes and make them easy to prepare? It was a thought that lay dormant in my mind for years.

Being of Arab origin, I have been familiar with Middle Eastern foods all my life. On the western Canadian prairies where I grew up as a child during the Depression years, our family survived and, food-wise, thrived, due to the Arab meals that my mother prepared—the same dishes eaten in the Middle East since the dawn of civilization. When our neighbors could not make ends meet and, one after another, were compelled to move away, we survived on tasty dishes made from broad beans, chickpeas, lentils, and vegetables, all grown in our hand-watered garden. In the ensuing years, when the Depression was only a memory, I still remembered my mother's dishes, which I began to simplify and prepare. When I was young and lived at home, I often heard my sisters say that even though they loved Arab food, when they grew up they would never cook it. "It's too much work," was their refrain. Subsequently, as I raised a family and roamed across Canada and beyond, I heard the phrase, "It's too much work," or at other times, "It's too complicated," from hundreds of the descendants of Arab immigrants.

My experience when it came to other Asian foods was the same. Growing up in southern Saskatchewan, I had no idea about other Asian food. In the village near our farm was a Chinese gentleman who had a small restaurant. He was the only person from the Far East that I had ever seen. He served regular Canadian fare—and no one knew what he himself ate. Without doubt he would have been broke in a few weeks should he have served Chinese food. Foreigners were not among the most-loved people at that time. Even immigrants like our family would not have eaten strange food. Like most newcomers with inferiority complexes, we wanted to become "real" Canadians by rejecting everything from our past. The rare times we had other Canadians dine in our home, my mother would never dream of making Arab food for them. In her mind and the minds of many other immigrants, the foods of their homelands could not be good enough for those they thought to be superior.

The first time I encountered the other foods of Asia was at a Chinese restaurant in Regina, the capital of Saskatchewan. It was a totally different food experience! The noodle and rice dishes that my friends and I enjoyed that day—with their sauces and meat and vegetables—were my introduction to the Asian culinary world. This meal and countless subsequent others made me a lover of the foods of Asia. As I traveled across Canada in the ensuing years, I would always search for a Chinese restaurant. The food of that ancient land had become my ultimate culinary love. As the years passed and Toronto became my home, a new gastronomic world opened before me. New immigrants began to pour into the city after World War II, and a good number of these opened restaurants serving the food of their homelands. Gone were the days when my mother would butcher a chicken to roast for a visiting neighbor, not wanting to feed them the food she was cooking for our family that day. Canadians began searching for new and exotic foods,

and the restaurants serving foreign foods thrived.

Mongolian to Moroccan and all the foods in between can now be found in Toronto. Indeed, there is a saying in the city that if one wishes to try a new ethnic food each day of the year, one would not run out of restaurants. A whole world of foods is now available in a country that during my youth served virtually no foreign food. I can now honestly say that I live in culinary heaven: Toronto has welcomed the foods of the world.

In later years, when I traveled in the Far East countries of China, Indonesia, Malaysia, Singapore, Thailand, and others, my horizon expanded to include all the foods of Asia.

My trip to China was highlighted by the city of Xi'an, where China had its real beginning. Xi'an was the first stop on the famous Silk Road, where the caravans began their journeys westward, then returned, bringing with them the foods of India, Persia, the Arab world, and beyond— many of which were incorporated into the Xi'an kitchen, creating a unique and tasty cuisine. Here, as I relished the succulent barbecues and seemingly endless Jiaozis (dumplings)—in my view part of one of the top cuisines in China— I remembered my boyhood friends who believed that the lone Chinese restaurant owner did not know good food until he came to Canada and learned to make hamburgers. "If they only knew what they missed in life!" I thought to myself, as I bit into another shrimp-filled dumpling.

My trips to the Far East and the Middle East, as well as my forays into Toronto's ethnic culinary world, gave me the urge to begin cooking my own Asian foods. Through the years I leafed through endless cookbooks, noting that the majority of recipes appeared complicated and would put off a novice. Add to that stumbling block the fact that some of the ingredients were virtually unavailable in North America, and my sisters' words, "It's too complicated" rang in my ears.

"What's the problem?" I thought to myself. "I will just re-create the recipes so that no one can say they are too complicated."

Asian Condiments

Below is a list of some of the condiments that may be unfamiliar in the Western kitchen. All of these listed here have been used in the recipes. The entries provide a general description of them and, in some cases, possible substitutes if the condiment is unavailable.

Ajowan or Ajwain Seed—A spice popular in Indian foods such as bean dishes, biscuits, breads, and pastries. Called *al-kamun al-muluki* ("cumin of the king") by the Arabs, it is much used in the vegetarian foods found in southern India. When crushed, the seeds have a strong thyme-like aroma. Therefore, thyme can be used as a substitute.

Aleppo or Halaby Pepper—Grown in northern Syria and Turkey, these semi-hot red chiles are sun-dried, seeded, and ground. Aleppo peppers add zest and aroma to innumerable meat and vegetable dishes. If not available, 4 parts sweet paprika to 1 part cayenne pepper is a good substitute.

Bagoong—A fish or shrimp fermented paste that is a common ingredient used in the Philippine kitchen as an enhancing agent, replacing salt, soy sauce, or MSG. In taste and aroma similar to anchovy paste, it is used to make fish stock, a dressing for steamed greens, and a condiment and dipping sauce. If not available, anchovy paste or soy sauce make good substitutes.

Baharat—A mixture of finely ground spices used to season lamb, beef, and chicken. The blend varies depending upon the region. In the Arab countries of the Middle East, it is typically a mixture of allspice, black pepper, cinnamon, nutmeg, ginger, cloves, and cardamom. In the countries surrounding the Arabian Gulf, the mixture may consist of black pepper, chili, paprika, and a small amount of cardamom, cinnamon, cloves, coriander, and cumin, used mostly when cooking meat. *Baharat* can be pur-

chased in any Middle Eastern grocery. China has its own compound of mixed spices called Chinese Five-Spice Powder, made from cinnamon, cloves, fennel seeds, star anise, and Szechuan peppercorns. Similar mixtures, using chili instead of Szechuan peppercorns, can be substituted.

Banana Ketchup (or Banana Sauce)—In the Philippines, instead of tomatoes, bananas are used to prepare ketchup. It is commercially produced in the Philippines both for domestic consumption and for export. Banana ketchup is perfect with fried chicken, barbecue pork, Philippine egg rolls, and numerous other foods. If not available, tomato ketchup can be used as a substitute.

Belacan—*See Shrimp Paste.*

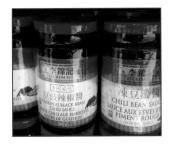

Black Bean Sauce—Made from fermented black beans, this is a subtle and savory sauce used for marinating and stir-frying, adding zest to vegetables, noodles, and meats. More a cooking ingredient than a condiment, it is used in regional Chinese cuisines. Available in Asian groceries and in the international sections of most grocery stores, black bean sauce can also be purchased flavored with garlic, ginger, red pepper flakes, or spices.

Black Cumin (or Black Caraway, *Nigella Sativa*, or *Kolonji*, or *Kashmiri cumin* in India)—Cumin has been used in Asia for untold centuries for its medicinal qualities. It is a popular spice used in traditional North Indian, Pakistani, Arab, and Iranian dishes. In Indian cooking, it is used to season meat and vegetable dishes. Stir-frying the seeds in oil or toasting them releases their flavor. Sprinkling them on food toward the end of the cooking process adds a smoky, peppery taste and crunchy texture. Cumin seeds

can be used as a substitute, but they do not give the same taste. In Kashmiri cuisine, black cumin is an essential ingredient in meat and rice dishes.

Chinese Plum Sauce—
A sweet and sour tasting sauce, it is both a table condiment and an ingredient in numerous Chinese dishes. Perfect as a glaze, a dipping sauce, and a barbecue sauce, it also enhances dishes such as

barbecued ribs, roast pork, boiled shrimp, egg rolls, and much more. If not available, hoisin sauce can be used as a substitute.

Chutney (also known as *Chatni, Bajji,* and *Gojju*)—A name used for a variety of sweet and spicy condiments, made from fresh, chopped fruit or vegetables mixed with seasonings. There are innumerable types of chutneys, such as mint and pineapple chutneys. However, one of the most common is mango chutney, a hot, sweet, and spicy condiment. In the Indian subcontinent, chutney is used in the same fashion as salsa is used in Latin American cuisine, or as relish is used in the kitchens of North America and Europe. Chutneys always form an integral part of the daily meal—if absent, the meal is incomplete. This excellent food enhancer goes well with meat dishes such as kebabs and other barbecued foods.

Curry Powder—Usually prepared from a variety of spices that include all or any combination of these spices: cardamom, cinnamon, cloves, coriander seeds, cumin, chilli powder, fenugreek, ginger, mustard seeds, paprika, saffron, and turmeric. If a ready-made curry

powder is not available, prepare a mixture from these ingredients. *See Garam Masala.*

Dashi—A Japanese cooking stock used in soups, broths, stews, and other Japanese dishes. *Dashi* is made from dried kelp, dried bonito, dried sardines, or the vegetarian type made from dried shiitake mushrooms. It is available in Asian markets in powdered or paste form.

Dried shrimp—*See Shrimp, dried.*

Fish Sauce—Consists of a wide range of types and is one of the most common ingredients used in Southeast Asian cuisines. It is prepared from fermented fish and is

used in seafood, soup, and vegetable dishes in place of salt. If not available, substitute soy sauce.

Garam Masala—A popular northern Indian curry powder. It is one of the most popular curries used in the Indian subcontinent and beyond. A type favored in meat dishes is a mixture of cardamom, cinnamon, cloves, coriander seeds, and black pepper; another uses these spices but also includes bay leaves, cumin, and dried chiles. If not available, other curries can be used as a substitute.

Hoisin Sauce—One of China's top condiments, this rich and very tasty sauce is a bean sauce combined with chile peppers, garlic, salt, and various other spices and ingredients. At times it is referred to as barbecue sauce, but in flavor it is very different from other barbecue sauces. It is much favored by the Chinese as a marinade or paste

ingredient for grilled or roasted fowl and meat, especially when it comes to roast duck or spareribs. The sauce is also excellent when used for dipping (especially chicken), lightly spread over fries, or spooned over baked potatoes and rice. There is no need for substitutes since hoisin sauce is generally available in supermarkets.

Lemongrass—A very important ingredient in numerous Asian dishes, found in Asian food markets throughout North America and in many of the larger non-Asian supermarkets. It is a fragrant herb with the scent and flavor of lemons, and it is best when fresh. If fresh is unavailable, dried or powdered lemongrass can be used. Lemon rind or zest can be used as a substitute for flavor.

Mirin—A type of sweet rice wine, similar to *sake* but with less alcohol and more sugar, an essential in flavoring Japanese dishes and in adding shine to glazes and sauces. This can be purchased in Asian groceries and in the "International" section of some supermarkets. If not available, a good substitute is ¼ teaspoon sugar to ¼ cup white wine, or 1 teaspoon sugar dissolved with 1 tablespoon dry sherry, or 2 parts *sake* mixed with 1 part sugar.

Miso—A rich and salty traditional Japanese food/condiment, *miso* is the essence of Japanese cooking and comes in a wide variety of types. Although extensively used in Japan, in the last few decades its use has been spreading worldwide. It is produced by fermenting a grain such as barley, rice, or wheat with soybeans, salt, and a mold culture, then aging it in wooden kegs for a number of years. It is an ingredient in soups, marinades, salad dressings, sauces, spreads, and innumerable other foods, and it is used to replace salt, bouillon cubes, or soy sauce. To retain its flavor, *miso* should be added after the dishes are cooked, just before serving. In North America *miso* is sold in many natural and organic shops or Asian shops and some supermarkets. If not available, substitute soy sauce with a little lemon juice.

Mung Beans—These beans are sold whole, split, hulled, as flour, or even sprouted. They are considered very nutritious and the easiest of the legumes to digest. If unavailable, they can be substituted with green peas or lentils. Mung bean sprouts are one of the most widely used vegetables in numerous Eastern foods.

MSG (Monosodium Glutamate)—MSG is made of glutamate, which is found naturally in protein-containing foods such as meat, poultry, vegetables, and milk. It boosts the natural flavor of foods such as meat, poultry, seafood, and vegetables and in dishes such as soups, gravies, sauces, stews, and stir-fry dishes. Especially in Japan and China, MSG is a popular food additive. However, MSG has been known to cause mild to severe allergic reactions.

Nuoc Cham—A brownish Vietnamese fish sauce obtained by fermenting salted fresh anchovies with lime juice, sugar, chopped chiles, ginger, garlic, and fresh herbs. *Nuoc Cham* is similar to the Thai *nam pla*, but stronger in taste. Vietnamese *mam nem* or other anchovy-based sauces or pastes can be used as substitutes.

Nuoc Mam—*See Nuoc Cham.*

Orange Blossom Water (in Arabic, *ma' zahr*)—Distilled water that has been infused with essential oil extracted from the fragrant blossoms of the bitter Seville orange; it is favored in Arab, Indian, and Persian cooking. It is used primarily when preparing sweets or as an added taste to beverages. In Iran and India, a few drops added to a salad of greens or to chicken, lamb, or rice dishes give a unique flavor to the food. It is available at Middle Eastern and international food stores. If not available, substitute the somewhat milder rose water. Once opened, it should be stored in the refrigerator.

Oyster Sauce—Commonly used in Chinese (especially Cantonese), Philippine, Thai, and other Far East cuisines, oyster sauce comes in many varieties. One of the best is Lee Kum Kee Oyster Sauce, carrying the name of its nineteenth-century inventor. The traditional sauces are generally prepared from oysters, brine, flavor enhancers such as MSG, and most times preservatives that increase shelf life. However, there are oyster sauces made with wholly vegetarian ingredients such as mushrooms. All these sauces improve the flavor of gravies, soups, stir-fries, and vegetable dishes. One type of oyster sauce or another can be found in most supermarkets in North America.

Palm Sugar—Used in numerous Asian countries as a natural sweetening agent, it has a distinctive caramel flavor. Conventional sugar, even though a poor substitute, can be used as replacement.

Pandan Leaf—Found in almost every garden in Indonesia, Malaysia, Sri Lanka, and Thailand, this fragrant leaf is used for its aroma and color in desserts, soups, and rice. To perfume rice, a pandan leaf is usually released into the pot while the rice is cooking, or it is simmered with curry to give a delicate and appealing scent to the dish. To give flavor and color to cakes and sweets, the leaves are pounded and blended with a little water before adding to the other ingredients. Green food coloring may be substituted simply for the color, but not for the flavor.

Patis—A strong fish sauce made from fish fermented with salt, *patis* is one of the most important condiments in Philippine cooking. Both a flavoring and a condiment, *patis* is a clear, amber-colored sauce used in Philippine cooking as much as soy sauce is used in Chinese cuisine. If not available, soy sauce or salt alone may be substituted.

Pickled Ginger—Best known as a condiment with sushi, it is ginger root sliced paper-thin and pickled in vinegar with red shiso leaves and salt. It is known in Japan as *gari* and is also used as a garnish. It is available in Asian markets.

Pomegranate Syrup (in Arabic, *dibs rumman*)— A pomegranate syrup or molasses-like concentrate, it is much used in Arab and western Asian cuisine. It is prepared by boiling pomegranate juice until it becomes thick and turns brownish. The condensed juice is used to make drinks

or to give soups, stews, and sauces a pleasing and somewhat tart taste. Utilized in meat pies, stuffings, and barbecues, pomegranate syrup enhances the taste of meat. If the concentrate is not available, use grenadine syrup or lemon juice as a substitute.

Rose Water (in Arabic, *ma' ward*; in Persian, *golab*; in India, *gulab jal*)—Made from purified water and distilled essence of roses, it has been used in cosmetics and perfumery as well as medicine for centuries. However, in the Middle East and many Asian countries, it has long been used as a flavoring agent in food. It is an ingredient in many Arab, Persian, Indian, and Turkish sweets such

as custards, ice creams, pastries, puddings, and candies. A good example is marzipan and Turkish delight, as well as sweet drinks. If not available, substitute orange blossom water.

Shoyu—A type of soy sauce that is the foundation of Japanese cuisine. It is made from fermented soybeans, roasted wheat, sea salt, and water. If not available, substitute soy sauce.

Shrimp, dried—Common to many Far Eastern countries, dried shrimp come under different names such as the Vietnamese *tom kho*. These are dried and salted shrimp used to season a number of dishes such as soup and stir-fries. Shrimp are soaked about an hour before use, and the liquid in which they were soaked is reserved and used to give a tasty tinge to soups and sauces. If not available, substitute pureed fresh shrimp.

Shrimp Paste (in Malay, *belacan*)—Also known as *belachan*, *blachang*, or *balachong*; *terasi*, *trassi*, or *terasie* in Indonesian; *kapi* in Thai and the Lao language; *mam tom* in Vietnamese; and *bagoong* or *alamang* in Tagalog, it is one of the important condiments that gives the cuisine of the Far East its renowned flavor. This hot and salty shrimp paste is an essential ingredient in many curries and sauces. It keeps well for a long time without refrigeration.

Soy Sauce—Soy sauce has been known in China for about 2,000 years. When it comes to the cuisines of the Far East, soy sauce is the prime ingredient in the kitchen—more essential than any other condiment. The sauce is traditionally made from soybeans mixed with roasted grain such as wheat, rice, or barley and fermented for several months, then strained and bottled. However, today some soy sauces often include other ingredients, while others are synthetically manufactured in a few days. However, they cannot match the real product. Two types of soy sauces are usually found: light, with a light color and salty flavor; and dark, more aged and with a thicker

texture. With the exception of desserts, soy sauce is used with almost all other dishes, from rice, fish, and all types of meat and vegetable entrées to appetizers, casseroles, dips, soups, and stews. A variety of soy sauces are found in all food markets in North America, even in the smaller towns.

Sumac or Sumach—

An important red berry-spice in western Asian cooking, usually sold dried and ground. It has a pleasantly fruity, sharp-sour taste that gives a tang to fish, meat, poultry, and vegetables, especially certain types of Middle

Eastern salads. Sprinkled over appetizers and other food such as cooked rice and yogurt dishes, it decorates the dishes while at the same time adding much to their taste. There really is no spice that can compare to it. If not available, lemon or lime juice or pomegranate syrup can be used as a substitute. Sumac is available in Middle Eastern grocery stores and some stores that specialize in international organic foods.

Tahini—

A sesame seed paste used as a flavoring ingredient in Middle Eastern dishes—its most famous contribution to the culinary world is to the dish *hummus bi tahini* (popularly known in the Western world as hummus) and *baba ghannouj*, a grilled eggplant appetizer. Tahini's subtle and smooth taste and versatility make it an ideal

base for innumerable sauces. Peanut butter can be used as a replacement, but it cannot compare to what this western Asian sauce has to offer.

Tamarind Paste—

Made from the tamarind fruit and ready to use as a cooking paste. It contains a good amount of tartaric acid, making it very sharp in taste. Commonly used in Indian curries and chutneys as a souring agent, it is also popular in other

Asian countries, as well as some Mediterranean countries and Mexican dishes. If not available, pomegranate syrup, sumac, or lemon juice can be used as substitutes.

Teriyaki—

A Japanese sauce made from a mixture of soy sauce, *sake* or *mirin*, sugar, ginger, and seasonings. The most common use of the sauce is as a marinade for all types of fish, meats, and some vegetables that are then broiled, fried, or grilled, giving a delicious baste for items hot off the grill. A sweet

and sour sauce or a mixture of soy sauce and French dressing can be used as a substitute.

Thai sweet basil—

A common basil in Thailand, it has purplish stems and green leaves, and it imbues an aniseed aroma and flavor. Use it in curries, soups, and stir-fries. If not available, it can be replaced with other types of basil and a tiny bit of aniseed.

Wasabi Paste—

A product made from a type of horseradish only grown in Japan, wasabi is somewhat hotter than the familiar white horseradish. It is also available in powder form. Both paste and powder have a sharp flavor and can be used instead of chiles. Wasabi paste

can also be used as a replacement for Dijon mustard.

CHAPTER 1

Filipino Food

A LEGACY FROM A MÉLANGE OF CULTURES

A meal in the Philippine Islands is a satisfying culinary adventure, whether served at home, at sidewalk food stands, or in plush restaurants. The food is exotic, somewhat spicy, tangy, and colorful. Historically, many peoples and cultures have contributed to this cuisine, a unique blend of Eastern and Western cooking that is reflected in the Filipino kitchen today.

The Malays, the original people on the islands, came to the Philippines some 20,000 years ago. In the ensuing centuries, the Chinese, Arab, and Indian traders, as well as the Spanish, American, and Japanese conquerors, all had a marked impact on the cuisine of this island archipelago.

From among the many Chinese contributions were soy products, stir-frying, deep-frying, and noodle dishes that the Filipinos adapted to their own taste.

The Spaniards came with an entirely new cuisine, such as sausages, thick stews, baked goods, and elaborate desserts. They introduced garlic and tomatoes and the method of sautéing them with onions in olive oil. As the ruling class, their cuisine predominated, and their kitchen became that of the wealthy. It is said that about 80 percent of the dishes prepared in the Philippines today can be traced back to the Spanish kitchen. Dishes like mechado, pochero, relleno, ensaymada, pan de sal, and leche flan, easily identified by their Spanish names, remain today as luxury food, usually served on special occasions such as fiestas and at Christmas.

The Americans introduced salads, pies, and modern cooking utensils, as well as fast foods: hamburgers, hot dogs, and canned foods, adapting them to Filipino taste.

The Filipinos took on American canned foods, but imbued them with their own flavor. Chefs frying canned corn beef with garlic and onions have created a dish uniquely Filipino; hamburgers are served with garlic, onion, and soy sauce; and Kentucky Fried Chicken is not breaded here, but instead, chicken is marinated in garlic, soy sauce, and vinegar before frying.

Filipinos like their food somewhat sour and salty, and are partial to frying with garlic. Boiled fish in sour stock with vegetables and a savory sauce is a typical item on the Filipino menu. On the other hand, many cooks have a tendency to toss all sorts of ingredients into soups and stews. Rice is the most important of the basic foods in the Filipino diet. It is eaten every day, three times a day—a meal without rice is not considered a meal. The rice is usually boiled until fluffy, and leftover rice is often fried with garlic for breakfast. Rice is used as the main ingredient in a good number of the country's desserts as well. For the poor, a meal often consists of rice soaked in various sauces together with a few vegetables and a piece of fish. It is said that everything else Filipinos eat is only a condiment to enhance the rice.

Next to rice, all types of creatures of the sea are on the menu, especially for coastal inhabitants.

With 7,107 islands forming the longest discontinuous coastline of any country in the world, seafood is very important in providing protein in the Philippines. Before outside influences crept into their cuisine, the Filipinos' food included everything fresh that nature had to offer, especially the "fruits of the sea." They preferred their seafood fresh and crawling out of the cook pot.

Most restaurants in the country offer fish and seafood dishes prepared in countless ways. The abundant fish, crab, oysters, rock lobsters, shrimp, and squid have given the country great dishes based on the "larder of the sea."

A main feature in Filipino cooking is the combination of various meats, such as chicken and shrimp, or fish and pork. The dishes prepared with these and other meats are made more appetizing by the skillful use of coconut milk, garlic, ginger, and onions, as well as tropical fruits such as guava, mango, and tamarind.

Savory sauces, on the other hand, give the Filipino cuisine its uniqueness. Bagoong, a shrimp paste, is used extensively, as is soy sauce, especially as a stewing sauce for chicken and pork. Filipino cooks also have a sauce made from crushed garlic and vinegar.

Of course, traveling to the Philippines and partaking of the country's cuisine is the ideal way in which to enjoy the country's food. However, should one wish to enter the Filipino culinary world without visiting the country, the following recipes are a good substitute. These dishes are fairly traditional, and preparation, even by an amateur, should be no problem. Many chefs who know Filipino cooking say that it is easy— and my recipes are easier still.

Sinangag
Eggs and Peas Fried Rice

Serves about 4

5 garlic cloves, crushed

2 tablespoons cooking oil

1 medium onion, thinly sliced

1 tablespoon grated fresh ginger

2 cups cooked medium- or long-grain white rice

1 cup fresh or frozen peas

2 eggs, beaten

2 tablespoons soy sauce

¼ teaspoon salt

½ teaspoon black pepper

Stir-fry garlic in cooking oil over medium-high heat for 1 minute. Add onion and ginger, then stir-fry for 3 minutes. Add rice, peas, and eggs, then stir-fry for 3 minutes. Stir in remaining ingredients, then serve hot.

Shrimp in Garlic

Serves about 4

5 tablespoons butter

6 garlic cloves, crushed

½ small hot pepper, seeded and finely chopped

1 pound peeled and deveined shrimp, thawed

½ teaspoon salt

¼ teaspoon black pepper

4 tablespoons finely chopped fresh cilantro or parsley

In a frying pan, melt butter over low heat then sauté garlic and hot pepper over medium heat until garlic begins to brown. Add shrimp, then sprinkle with salt and pepper. Stir-fry for a further 5 to 6 minutes. Stir in cilantro or parsley, and serve sizzling hot.

Sinigang — Shrimp Soup

Serves about 8

6 cups water

2 medium onions, finely chopped

4 medium tomatoes, chopped

1 cup (1-inch cut) trimmed string beans

1 small hot pepper, seeded and finely chopped

4 garlic cloves, crushed

1 tablespoon tamarind paste, dissolved in 1 cup warm water

2 tablespoons fish sauce

1 teaspoon salt

1 pound raw shrimp, unpeeled and deveined

1 (10-ounce) package spinach, thoroughly washed and chopped

Place water, onions, and tomatoes in a saucepan and bring to boil. Cover and cook over medium heat for 15 minutes. Add beans, hot pepper, garlic, tamarind-water solution, fish sauce, and salt, then re-cover and cook over low heat for 10 minutes. Add shrimp, re-cover, and cook for a further 8 minutes. Turn off heat and add spinach. Cover and let stand for 10 minutes.

ASIAN COOKING MADE SIMPLE

Rellenong Manok — Baked Stuffed Chicken

Serves 4 to 6

Marinade:

4 tablespoons soy sauce

1 tablespoon sugar

3 tablespoons lemon juice

3 to 4 pounds whole chicken, washed

Stuffing:

¼ pound ground ham

¼ pound sausage, cut into small pieces

½ cup shredded cheddar cheese

4 tablespoons bread crumbs

1 medium onion, finely chopped

5 garlic cloves, crushed

1 egg, beaten

2 tablespoons raisins

2 tablespoons sweet relish

1 teaspoon salt

½ teaspoon black pepper

½ cup water

4 tablespoons butter, melted

Gravy:

2 tablespoons white flour

1 teaspoon garlic powder

In the Philippines, the chicken used in this recipe is de-boned without piercing the skin, but due to the considerable work this entails, I have used a whole chicken.

For the marinade:

⟩ *Combine 3 tablespoons of the soy sauce, sugar, and lemon juice, then rub chicken with mixture and marinate for 3 to 4 hours.*

For the stuffing:

⟩ *Combine ham, sausage, cheddar cheese, bread crumbs, onion, garlic, egg, raisins, relish, salt, pepper, and water to make stuffing.*

⟩ *Preheat oven to 350° F.*

⟩ *Stuff the chicken, both back and neck, then sew closed with cotton kitchen twine. Rub with butter, then place in a roasting pan and cover. Roast for 2 hours, basting every 30 minutes from the pan juices, then remove cover and continue roasting for 15 minutes or until chicken turns golden brown.*

For the gravy:

⟩ *Take out drippings from the roaster and place in a small saucepan, then add flour, garlic powder, and the remaining 1 tablespoon of soy sauce. Stir-fry while adding a little water to make gravy.*

Ukoy — Shrimp Fritters

Serves about 6

2 cups bean sprouts

1½ cups chopped raw shrimp

1 cup white flour

2 eggs, beaten

½ cup finely chopped fresh cilantro

½ cup finely chopped green onion

4 garlic cloves, crushed

1 teaspoon salt

½ teaspoon black pepper

½ teaspoon red chili flakes

Water

Oil

Combine in a mixing bowl all ingredients except water and oil. Then stir in as much water as needed to create a pancake-like batter. Place oil to about a 1 inch depth in a saucepan, then heat. Drop heaping tablespoons of batter in oil, then fry over medium heat until fritters become golden brown. Drain on paper towels, then serve warm.

Adobong Manok
Chicken with Vinegar

Serves about 6

4 tablespoons cooking oil

1 chicken (about 4 pounds), cut into serving pieces

1 garlic head, peeled and crushed

½ cup white vinegar

5 tablespoons soy sauce

1½ teaspoons pepper

6 bay leaves

¼ cup water

Considered to be the Philippines' national dish, this Spanish-influenced dish is simple to prepare.

Heat oil in a saucepan, then fry chicken and garlic over medium-low heat for 10 minutes, turning chicken pieces over once. Add remaining ingredients and bring to boil, then cover and cook over medium-low heat for 40 minutes or until chicken is well done, turning pieces over once and adding a little water if necessary. Serve chicken pieces with sauce and accompanied by cooked rice.

Lumpia – Fried Spring Rolls

Makes 20 rolls

Filling:

4 tablespoons cooking oil
1 pound ground beef
¼ pound cooked medium shrimp
1 medium onion, finely chopped
5 garlic cloves, crushed
1 cup finely chopped mushrooms
1 cup finely chopped potatoes
2 tablespoons soy sauce
2 teaspoons oyster sauce
1 teaspoon fish sauce
½ teaspoon black pepper

1 (10-ounce, 20-wrapper) package spring roll wrappers
Oil for deep frying

For the filling:

Heat oil in a frying pan, then sauté beef over medium heat for 10 minutes. Stir in remaining ingredients, except spring roll wrappers and oil, then stir-fry for a further 4 minutes to make filling.

To make the spring rolls:

Lay wrappers on a flat surface, then place about 2 heaping tablespoons of filling evenly across, 1 inch from each edge of wrapper. Fold edge over filling, then fold both ends over filling and roll into cigar shape. Moisten the last edge of the wrapper with dabs of water to seal. Repeat using the remainder of wrappers. Heat oil in a saucepan, then deep-fry lumpia for about 5 minutes or until golden brown, turning over once. Serve with dipping sauce.

Pancit – Shrimp and Noodles

Serves about 6

½ pound thin noodles (any type)
4 tablespoons cooking oil
1 large onion, finely chopped
4 garlic cloves, crushed
1 tablespoon grated fresh ginger
4 cups shredded Chinese cabbage
2 cups chopped cooked shrimp
3 tablespoons soy sauce
3 tablespoons oyster sauce
2 tablespoons water
⅛ teaspoon cayenne pepper
½ cup chopped green onion

This Chinese-inspired creation is another of the Philippines' traditional dishes. To spice it up a little, cayenne pepper has been added.

❯ *Prepare noodles according to directions on package, then set aside but keep warm.*
❯ *Heat oil in a frying pan, then add onion, garlic, and ginger. Stir-fry over medium-high heat for 3 minutes, then stir in cabbage, shrimp, soy sauce, oyster sauce, water, and cayenne pepper. Stir-fry for 3 more minutes.*
❯ *Place noodles on platter, then spoon frying pan contents over noodles. Garnish with green onion and serve.*

Morcon — Rolled Beef

Serves 4

1 pound beef round steak,
cut into 4 square pieces about ¼ inch thick

2 tablespoons soy sauce

2 beef sausages, cut in half lengthwise

1 medium carrot, thinly sliced lengthwise in 4 slices

2 sweet pickles, cut in half lengthwise

2 hard-boiled eggs, sliced

½ cup shredded cheddar cheese

1 beef bouillon cube, dissolved in 1 cup hot water

2 tablespoons butter, melted

½ teaspoon garlic powder

½ teaspoon black pepper

Fresh parsley (optional)

> Marinate beef in soy sauce for 1 to 2 hours.
> Preheat oven to 350° F.
> Spread beef squares on a flat surface. On one edge of each of the squares place sausage, carrot, pickle, eggs, and cheese, evenly divided. Roll tightly into cigar shape, then place in a baking dish with seams down and set aside.
> Combine remaining ingredients, except parsley, and pour over beef rolls. Cover and bake for 45 minutes. Uncover and bake for a further 15 minutes.
> Slice morcon and arrange on a platter. Spoon juice from baking dish over top, then garnish with parsley (optional) and serve hot.

Palitaw — Boiled Rice Cookies

Makes 2 dozen cookies

2 cups rice flour

1 cup water

1 teaspoon vanilla extract

Extra water

½ cup finely grated coconut

½ cup sugar

4 tablespoons sesame seeds

½ teaspoon cinnamon

> Knead flour with water and vanilla extract, adding more water or flour if necessary. Form into 24 balls, then flatten into oval shape and set aside.
> Fill half of a small saucepan with water, then bring to boil.
> Drop shaped balls in boiling water 3 to 4 at a time. Remove immediately with a slotted spoon when the shaped balls float to top, and drop each in cold water. Make sure that they are removed as soon as they float. If left cooking too long, they will become hard. Let stand in cold water for a few minutes.
> Combine coconut, sugar, sesame seeds, and cinnamon and place in a plate. Drain cookies and roll in the mixture. Serve immediately.

CHAPTER 2

Singapore Foods

A WORLD OF CULINARY DELIGHTS

Singapore is considered the melting pot of Asia, with a world-class cuisine. Offering a diverse menu encompassing Chinese, Indian, Malay, and European foods, as well as some very unique blends of these dishes, this country is a gourmet's paradise. The problem is not in finding fine foods, but deciding what to eat. With a staggering array of dishes, the pleasure of Singapore cuisine is a culinary delight not to be found in many other countries. For many centuries, Singapore was a major crossroad for the ancient eastern spice route. The English adventurer Sir Thomas Stamford Raffles bought the island from a Malay sultan and founded this tiny nation of 3 million people. Singapore, just off the southern tip of the Malaysia Peninsula, gets its name from Singa-Pura, Sanskrit for Lion City. As a whole, Singapore is a Chinese town with a strong Western face, mellowed by other influences. Its architecture is an eclectic mix of Colonial, Chinese, Malay, Indian, and Arab.

It is the same potpourri in communication and speech. The state has four official languages: Bahasa Malaysia (the national tongue), Mandarin, Tamil, and English, which is the language of business and administration. Even though 77 percent of the population is Chinese with various portions of Malayans, Indians, Eurasians, and others, English unites them all.

The country is a mixture of the great Asian cultures, but there is little friction between the religions. Buddhist and Hindu temples, Christian churches, Muslim mosques, and relics from the British colonial past all are respected in a live-and-let-live atmosphere.

This conglomeration has spawned a mind-boggling array of dishes that consist of Malaysian, Thai, all types of European foods, Asian peasant fare, and the courtly foods of Imperial China and India. The whole state is a miniature world of Asian cuisine, peppered by aspects of the Western kitchen. Everyone has access to these foods in the inexpensive, hygienic food courts found everywhere.

Arabs, Chinese, Malayans, Indians, and Europeans all played a part in bringing diversity to every aspect of life, especially when it came to the nation's cuisine. Today, Singapore presents the whole of Southeast Asia's culinary world in a microcosm.

Singapore is a cosmopolitan city-state where varied peoples came to appreciate each other's cooking. Each culture brought with it unique cooking methods. The new generations grew up and experimented with the new dishes brought in by the immigrants and, in the process, created a good number of unique Singaporean recipes. It is said that no other Asian country has such a wide array of dishes, a kaleidoscopic world of food. Because of Singapore's multiracial melting pot, all the immigrant cuisines compete in the battle of the taste buds, allowing the island's foods to reach a high standard of excellence proudly known to the island inhabitants as "Singapore Food," a fusion of Western and Asian cooking.

Peranakan or Nonya food is the closest that

Singapore has to an indigenous cuisine. The dishes are a combination of Chinese (mostly Cantonese), Malaysian, and other foods developed in a unique, imaginative, and extremely subtle Singapore blend. Regional Indian creations such as roti prata, rojak salad, and mutton soup; and versions of satay and mee goreng are now well-known Peranakan dishes. Other dishes, such as fish head curry, nasi lemak (a Malaysian rice dish with fish), chicken biryani (an Indian treat), and Hainanese chicken rice are found in hawker centers and food courts throughout the entire island.

A large segment of the population in Singapore is Muslim and, hence, halal food is found throughout this city-state. There are Arab, Indian, and Malaysian Muslim foods, also called Mamak food, that is almost always displayed with Arabic plaques. Nasi padang, a Muslim food originating from the island of Sumatra, in Indonesia, is one of these foods that every visitor should try.

Seafood prepared in a wide variety of ways is much favored by local inhabitants. Barbecued stingray, black pepper crabs, chile crab, deep-fried baby squid, and prawns are some of the seafood that Singaporeans cherish.

For visitors dining in world-class food establishments or in "hawker center" food courts, Singapore is the gourmet experience of a lifetime. The island nation has more than 500 fine restaurants that cater to every taste. They serve all types of cuisine, from American, Greek, and Italian to Korean, Japanese, Mexican, and northern Indian. Visit in July for a gastronomic treat, the Singapore Food Festival, a monthlong celebration of Singapore's gourmet food. However, if one cannot travel to Singapore, these few traditional dishes, prepared with easy-to-find ingredients, will provide an idea of the rich Singaporean cuisine.

Rojak — Singapore Salad

Serves 6 to 8

Sauce:
1 tablespoon seeded and finely chopped fresh chile pepper
1 tablespoon tamarind paste
1 tablespoon shrimp paste
1 tablespoon oyster sauce
3 tablespoons firmly packed brown sugar
⅓ cup water

1 medium cucumber (6 to 7 inches), peeled, quartered, and thinly sliced
2 cups diced pineapple
1 cup diced mango
1 cup diced papaya
1 cup boiled cuttlefish, thinly sliced
4 tablespoons coarsely ground roasted peanuts

For the sauce:
Place chile, tamarind paste, shrimp paste, oyster sauce, brown sugar, and water in a small saucepan and thoroughly mix. Cook over low heat until sugar dissolves and sauce becomes somewhat thick. Set aside and let cool.

Place the remaining ingredients, except peanuts, in a salad bowl, then gently mix. Stir in sauce, then garnish with peanuts and serve immediately.

Singapore Noodles

Serves about 8

½ pound fine egg noodles

1 tablespoon light sesame oil

3 tablespoons peanut oil

1 tablespoon grated fresh ginger

2 teaspoons curry powder

1 medium onion, finely sliced

½ pound bean sprouts

2 cups finely sliced mushrooms

1 cup shredded cabbage

2 cups shredded cooked chicken

2 tablespoons oyster sauce

1 tablespoon soy sauce

> Cook noodles according to directions on package, then drain. Mix with sesame oil and set aside.

> Heat a heavy frying pan or wok to piping hot, then add peanut oil, ginger, and curry powder. Stir-fry for a few seconds, then add onion, bean sprouts, mushrooms, and cabbage. Stir-fry for about 3 minutes. Stir in chicken and noodles, then stir-fry for 1 minute. Stir in oyster sauce and soy sauce, then serve hot.

Mutton Soup

Serves 6 to 8

1 pound mutton ribs with bones, cut into pieces

2 medium onions, chopped

4 garlic cloves, crushed

1 fresh large chile pepper, seeded and thinly sliced

1 teaspoon salt

2 tablespoons grated fresh ginger

8 cups water

3 tablespoons peanut oil

1 tablespoon curry powder

¼ teaspoon ground coriander seeds

¼ teaspoon ground cardamom

¼ teaspoon black pepper

½ cup chopped green onion

4 tablespoons finely chopped fresh cilantro

> Place mutton ribs, onions, garlic, chile, salt, 1 tablespoon of the ginger, and water in a saucepan, then bring to boil. Reduce to low heat, then cover and simmer for 2 hours or until mutton is tender. Remove mutton with a slotted spoon, but retain stock. Remove meat from bones, then cut into small pieces and set aside.

> Heat oil in a saucepan, then add remainder of ginger, curry powder, coriander, cardamom, and pepper. Stir-fry for 1 minute. Add the reserved stock and cooked mutton and bring to boil. Reduce to low heat, then cover and simmer for 20 minutes. Transfer to serving bowl. Stir in green onion and cilantro and serve.

Hot Peanut Sauce

Makes 1 to 1½ cups

4 tablespoons crunchy peanut butter

3 tablespoons lime juice

3 tablespoons white vinegar

2 tablespoons soy sauce

4 tablespoons finely chopped fresh cilantro

¼ teaspoon cayenne pepper

½ cup water

In a saucepan, warm peanut butter over low heat, then stir in remaining ingredients, adding more water if a thinner sauce is desired. Stir and boil for a few minutes, then serve with all types of meats and vegetables. Leftover sauce can be refrigerated for up to 3 days.

Chile Crabs

Serves about 4

Sauce:

2 tablespoons tomato paste

2 tablespoons soy sauce

1 tablespoon sugar

2 teaspoons cornstarch

1 cup water

4 tablespoons vegetable oil

6 large garlic cloves, crushed

3 fresh medium chile peppers, seeded and finely chopped

2 tablespoons grated fresh ginger

1½ pounds cooked crab legs, each broken into 2 pieces

1 tablespoon lime juice

1 cup (1-inch-cut pieces) green onion

4 tablespoons finely chopped fresh cilantro

Versions of this dish are very popular among Singaporeans.

For the sauce:

Make a sauce by combining tomato paste, soy sauce, sugar, cornstarch, and water, then set aside.

Heat a heavy frying pan or wok on very high heat, then add oil, garlic, chiles, and ginger. Stir-fry for 1 minute. Add crab legs, then stir-fry for a further 2 minutes. Stir in sauce and bring to boil, then cover and cook over high heat for 5 minutes, stirring a few times. Stir in remaining ingredients and serve.

Lassi — Yogurt Drink

Serves about 4

2 cups plain yogurt

1 cup water

5 tablespoons honey

1 teaspoon rose or orange blossom water

Of Indian origin, this drink is very refreshing during the hot summer weather.

Place all ingredients in a blender and blend for a few moments. Serve with ice cubes or chilled.

Singapore Apple Dessert

Serves about 8

2 tablespoons butter

4 large apples, peeled, cored, and chopped into small pieces

4 tablespoons raisins

4 tablespoons coarsely ground walnuts

1 cup plain yogurt

4 tablespoons sugar

❯ *Melt butter over low heat in a frying pan, then cook apples until they become soft, adding more butter if necessary. Allow to cool.*
❯ *In a bowl, combine all other ingredients, then mix in the apple. Place in serving dishes, then chill and serve.*

Nasi Lemak — Steamed Coconut Rice

Serves about 6

1½ cups long-grain white rice, rinsed

1½ cups coconut milk

1½ cups water

½ teaspoon salt

Place all ingredients in a saucepan then bring to boil. Cook over medium heat until all the liquid is absorbed, stirring a number of times, then cover. Turn off heat and let stand on element for another 30 minutes to cook in its own steam. Serve as a side dish for all foods containing sauces.

Curried Shrimp

Serves about 6

6 tablespoons white flour
2 teaspoons curry powder
1 teaspoon garlic powder
1 teaspoon salt
¼ teaspoon cayenne pepper
2 pounds fresh shrimp, peeled and deveined
4 tablespoons vegetable oil
1 bunch green onions, cut into 1-inch pieces
2 tablespoons lemon juice
2 tablespoons finely chopped fresh cilantro

> *Combine flour, curry powder, garlic powder, salt, and cayenne pepper, then add shrimp and toss. Set aside.*
> *Place oil in frying pan or wok over high heat, then stir-fry green onions for 1 minute. Add shrimp, then stir-fry for about 3 minutes or until shrimp are done. Place on a serving platter, then sprinkle with lemon juice. Decorate with cilantro and serve.*

Mee Goreng Mamak
Noodles with Potato and Seafood

Serves about 4

½ pound egg noodles
1 tablespoon light sesame seed oil
½ pound firm tofu, drained and diced into ½-inch cubes
1 cup cooking oil
6 garlic cloves, finely chopped
2 tablespoons grated fresh ginger
1 cup sliced cooked chicken
1 cup shredded cabbage
1 medium tomato, diced into ½-inch cubes
1 cup grated potatoes
½ pound bean sprouts
3 tablespoons tomato ketchup
2 tablespoons soy sauce
2 tablespoons oyster sauce
1 medium onion, sliced and fried
2 fresh red chile peppers, seeded and thinly sliced

> *Cook egg noodles according to package directions. Drain, then mix with 1 tablespoon sesame seed oil.*
> *In a saucepan, add ½ cup of the cooking oil and deep-fry tofu. Drain on paper towels and set aside.*
> *Heat remaining oil in a heavy frying pan or wok to piping hot, then add garlic and ginger and stir-fry for 1 minute. Stir in chicken and stir-fry for 1 minute. Add cabbage, tomato, potatoes, tofu, and bean sprouts, then stir-fry for 2 minutes. Stir in noodles, ketchup, soy sauce, and oyster sauce. Stir-fry for 1 more minute. Place on a serving platter, then garnish with onion and chiles and serve.*

CHAPTER 3
Rijsttafel
THE CROWN JEWEL OF INDONESIAN CUISINE

Indonesian cuisine is among the finest in the world, a rich and complex blend of many cultures. Chinese, Indian, Arab, Dutch, Spanish, Portuguese, and British preferences have influenced the development of the country's present-day foods. Above all, the cooking of Southeast Asia has had a profound impact. In the larger cities of the Indonesian archipelago, one can enjoy the chile peppers, peanut sauces, and stewed curries of Thailand; the lemongrass and fish sauce of Vietnam; the intricate spice combinations of India; and the endless dishes that are a combination of these foods. This culinary world of appetizing and exciting dishes reaches its epitome in the rijsttafel, the crown jewel of the Indonesian kitchen.

Indonesia, the fourth-most populous nation in the world, consists of some 13,000 islands that stretch from the island of Sumatra in the west to Papua New Guinea in the east. The Indonesian islands have been renowned for centuries as a center of rich international trade, especially in spices. For hundreds of years, cloves, ginger, mace, nutmeg, and black pepper drew traders from India, China, Africa, and the Arab world. Later, European explorers and colonists from the Netherlands, Portugal, and England came seeking these spices, and stayed on to colonize the land.

By the end of the sixteenth century, European colonial conquests had left the archipelago a collection of weak, disconnected fiefdoms, which were conquered by the Dutch within the next two centuries. Modern Indonesia only came into being after World War II.

A colorful nation, the country offers beautiful landscapes, a variety of natural wonders, ancient cultures, a fascinating mix of people, and delicious local cuisines that reflect the country's complex cultural history. A combination of many different influences, its cooking is somewhat different in the various regions and provinces, with Javanese and Sumatran dishes the most famous.

Strange as it may seem, cloves, mace, and nutmeg, which for hundreds of years formed the backbone of the spice trade, are rarely used in Indonesian culinary art. Coconut milk, used in beverages, sauces, soups, and rice, gives a distinctive taste to a good number of dishes. However, the fundamental spices of the country's cuisine are coriander seed, pepper, and garlic. Basil, bay leaves, cardamom, cassia, chile, ginger, galangal, lemongrass, peanuts, saffron, scallions, shallots, soy sauce, star anise, tamarind, turmeric, shrimp paste, and dried anchovies are often added to enhance these spices.

Some of the well-known Indonesian dishes are gado-gado (vegetables with peanut sauce), nasi goreng (fried rice with meat or seafood), sambals (various types of spice relishes), sateh (grilled skewers of meat served with a peanut sauce), and soto (soup). For ordinary people, a meal usually includes soup, salad, and a main dish that often consists of rice and dried fish, always accompanied by one or two sambals.

Steamed or boiled rice is always the centerpiece of a gourmet Indonesian meal, accompanied by numerous dishes of beef, chicken, duck, goat, all kinds of seafood, and vegetables. These can be boiled, grilled, roasted, steamed, stir-fried, or deep-fried, and they are served with several kinds of relishes and sauces.

Different areas in the archipelago offer their own distinctive dishes. In the province of West Sumatra, the Minangkabau region is well known for its spicy Padang food of Indian origin, featuring plenty of lamb curries and hot chiles. Restaurants usually display cooked food, prepared in the style of Padang, on some ten different plates and bowls in a glass box at the entrance. After visitors sit down to dine, the waiter brings a plate of rice and a plate of each of the dishes displayed; diners are charged only for the food they eat.

Javanese dishes feature delicate grilled and steamed seafood, and Bali is famous for its tasty dishes, some cooked with pork—the only part of Indonesia where visitors can find this meat. There are two excellent Balinese dishes that food-lovers should not miss: bebek betutu, a delicious duck specialty, slowly baked in banana leaves together with various herbs and spices, and sateh lilit, made from minced prawns and fish. These are served with nasi kuning (yellow rice).

Indonesia was once the richest agricultural region in the world. The Molucca Islands, a part of the Indonesian archipelago, were the original Spice Islands, supplying the entire world with black pepper, nutmeg, mace, and cloves.

The Dutch ruled here for 320 years, leaving an indelible mark on the country's cuisine. They are responsible for the rijsttafel (rice table) that originated with Dutch plantation owners who liked to sample selectively from Indonesian cuisine. It be-

came a kind of tradition, and the Dutch introduced it into the Netherlands. Today, the rijsttafel is a real culinary pleasure in both countries.

Called a forerunner of the all-you-can-eat Chinese buffet, rijsttafels at times feature more than 100 dishes. They are a great way to sample numerous Indonesian dishes, such as nasi kuning, loempia (egg rolls), sateh, perkedel (meatballs), sateh lilit, gado-gado, daging smoor (beef with soy sauce), babi ketjap (meat in soy sauce), kroepoek (shrimp toast), serundeng (fried coconut), roedjak manis (fruit in sweet sauce), and pisang goreng (fried banana), along with a number of sauces.

Rijsttafel is eaten by first placing a little of the hot rice in a soup bowl, then surrounding it with a little of the side dishes, as well as a small quantity of sambal on the edge of the plate to season the food. Each side dish has a special flavor of its own, so one should not mix the side dishes with the rice because the fine taste of the side dishes will be lost.

For the uninitiated, the mini rijsttafel that we have prepared below will be an exciting journey into the world of Indonesian food. For most of the recipes, I have suggested substitutes for various Indonesian ingredients that are not commonly available.

Sambal Iris
Vegetarian Condiment

Makes about 2 cups

2 medium onions, sliced in thin strips
1 large tomato, finely chopped
1 medium red hot pepper, seeded and cut into thin strips
1 fresh small green chile pepper, seeded and cut into thin strips
4 tablespoons finely chopped fresh basil
½ cup lemon juice
1 tablespoon lemon zest

Thoroughly combine all ingredients, then refrigerate for about 1 hour before serving with all types of meats and vegetables.

Sambal Kacang
Peanut Sauce

Makes about 1½ cups

2 tablespoons vegetable oil
2 garlic cloves, chopped
1 cup chopped green onion
1 tablespoon soy sauce
1 teaspoon shrimp paste
⅛ teaspoon cayenne pepper
½ teaspoon ground ginger
½ teaspoon firmly packed brown sugar
¼ teaspoon ground fennel seeds
1½ cups water
1 cup raw peanuts, lightly fried for
a few minutes, then finely ground
2 tablespoons lemon juice

A popular sauce served with sateh *and* Gado-Gado *(see below), this* sambal *goes well with all grilled meats and vegetables.*

Heat oil, then stir-fry garlic and green onion for 1 minute. Add remaining ingredients except peanuts and lemon juice. Bring to boil. Stir in peanuts, then simmer over low heat, stirring occasionally, for about 10 minutes or until sauce begins to thicken. Stir in lemon juice, then serve or allow to cool. Store in a jar in refrigerator.

Gado-Gado
Vegetables with Peanut Sauce

Serves 8 to 10

½ pound extra firm tofu, diced in ½-inch cubes
Cooking oil
2 cups shaved or grated carrots
1 cup shredded cabbage
2 cups snow peas
½ medium cucumber, thinly sliced
1 cup bean sprouts, washed
1 medium boiled potato, peeled and diced into ½-inch cubes
8 to 10 lettuce leaves
8 to 10 sprigs watercress
2 hard-boiled eggs, sliced
Sambal Kacang—Peanut Sauce (see above)

❯ *Stir-fry tofu in cooking oil until tofu begins to brown.*
❯ *In a mixing bowl, gently combine tofu and all ingredients except lettuce, watercress, and eggs. Set aside. If desired, stir-fry the mixing bowl contents for 2 minutes.*
❯ *Arrange the lettuce and watercress around the edge of a serving platter, then place the mixing bowl contents in middle of platter. Spread egg slices on top of the mixed vegetables. Cover salad to taste with Sambal Kacang Peanut Sauce (see above) or serve sauce as a side.*

Perkedel
Meat and Potato Patties

Serves 4

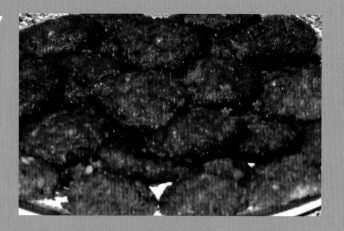

3 cups mashed potatoes
1 cup finely ground bread crumbs
1 cup ground meat (any type)
2 eggs, beaten
1 cup very finely chopped celery
1 medium onion, very finely chopped
2 garlic cloves, crushed
2 tablespoons finely chopped and seeded fresh chile pepper
3 tablespoons tomato ketchup
1 teaspoon salt
1 teaspoon ground coriander seeds
1 teaspoon ground cumin
1 teaspoon black pepper
¼ teaspoon nutmeg
Oil for deep-frying

Thoroughly combine all ingredients, except oil, then form into small patties. Deep-fry patties or place in well-greased baking pans, then bake in a 350° F preheated oven for 1 hour or until patties are well cooked. Serve warm with Sambal Kacang *(see page 31) and* Sambal Iris *(see page 30) sauces.*

Sateh Lilit
Barbecued Seafood

Serves about 8

1 pound fresh red snapper fillet
1 pound peeled and deveined fresh raw shrimp
2 cups freshly grated coconut
1 medium tomato, chopped
1 cup chopped green onion
6 garlic cloves, crushed
1 tablespoon grated fresh ginger
1 teaspoon ground coriander seeds
1 teaspoon black pepper
2 teaspoons salt
1 fresh chile pepper, seeded and very finely chopped
2 tablespoons firmly packed brown sugar
2 tablespoons lemon juice

Place snapper fillet and shrimp in a food processor and process for 1 minute. Add all remaining ingredients, then process for 1 more minute. Form mixture into spheres the size of golf balls, then form into rectangle shape. Place on wooden skewers and barbecue or place in a pan and broil until golden brown. Serve hot with peanut sauce.

Sateh Ajam — Broiled Chicken

Serves about 8

2 pounds chicken breast, cut into thin strips

5 garlic cloves, crushed

2 tablespoons peanut oil

2 tablespoons lemon juice

2 teaspoons fish sauce

⅛ teaspoon cayenne pepper

Sauce:

4 tablespoons vegetable oil

1 medium onion, finely chopped

2 tablespoons lime juice

2 tablespoons soy sauce

2 tablespoons sugar

2 tablespoons peanut butter

1 teaspoon ground coriander seeds

1 teaspoon ground cumin

½ teaspoon curry powder

½ teaspoon cinnamon

1 cup coconut milk

Place chicken strips in a bowl, then set aside.

For the marinade:
Place garlic, peanut oil, lemon juice, fish sauce, and cayenne pepper in a blender and blend for 1 minute. Pour mixture over chicken and marinate for a few hours.

For the dipping sauce:
Heat vegetable oil in a saucepan and fry onion over medium heat for 10 minutes. Stir in remaining ingredients, except coconut milk, and stir-fry for 2 minutes. Stir in coconut milk, then simmer over low heat for 5 minutes. Set aside.

Place chicken strips on skewers, then broil for about 5 minutes on each side or until chicken is done. Serve hot with dipping sauce.

Daging Smoor
Beef with Peanut Sauce

Serves 6

4 tablespoons vegetable oil
2 pounds tender lean beef, cut into pieces 1 x ½ inch
1 large onion, thinly sliced
4 garlic cloves, crushed
4 tablespoons sweet soy sauce
1 tablespoon grated fresh ginger
1 tablespoon firmly packed brown sugar
½ teaspoon black pepper
⅛ teaspoon cayenne pepper
2 cups water
2 tablespoons finely chopped lemongrass
1 small tomato, sliced
1 cucumber pickle, sliced
Sambal Kacang Peanut Sauce (see page 31)

Heat oil, then fry meat over medium heat until it begins to brown. Stir in remaining ingredients, except tomato, pickle, and peanut sauce, then bring to boil. Cover and simmer over medium-low heat for 40 minutes or until the meat is done, adding more water if necessary. Serve on a platter, garnished with tomato and pickle slices, along with peanut sauce.

Serundeng
Peanuts with Coconut

Serves about 6

6 tablespoons vegetable oil
2 cups raw peanuts
2 cups chopped green onion
3 garlic cloves, crushed
1 tablespoon shrimp sauce
1 teaspoon ground coriander seeds
½ teaspoon salt
½ teaspoon ground cumin
1 cup shredded coconut
1 teaspoon firmly packed brown sugar
2 tablespoons lemon juice
1 cup water

❯ *Heat oil in a frying pan, then fry peanuts over medium heat until they begin to brown. Remove peanuts from pan with a slotted spoon then allow to cool. Reserve oil in frying pan.*
❯ *Add to the reserved oil in frying pan remaining ingredients, except water, then stir-fry for a few minutes. Add water, then cover and simmer over low heat for 40 minutes or until water is completely absorbed, stirring frequently. Stir in peanuts, then allow to cool before serving.*

Nasi Kuning
Indonesian Yellow Rice

Serves 10 to 12

3 cups long-grain white rice, rinsed

3 cups coconut milk

3 cups water

1 tablespoon finely chopped fresh lemongrass

4 bay leaves

1 teaspoon turmeric

1 teaspoon salt

½ teaspoon black pepper

¼ teaspoon ground cloves

¼ teaspoon cinnamon

3 tablespoons butter

Place all ingredients, except butter, in a saucepan, then bring to boil. Simmer uncovered for 20 minutes over low heat or until all liquid has been absorbed, stirring a few times. Turn off heat and cover. Let sit for 30 minutes. Add butter and fluff, then place on a platter and serve hot.

Pisang Goreng
Banana Fritters

Serves about 8

Batter:

½ cup white flour

½ cup water

1 teaspoon baking powder

1 egg, beaten

½ teaspoon cinnamon

Oil for frying

4 large ripe bananas, peeled, halved lengthwise, and cut into 2- to 3-inch pieces

½ cup whipping cream

½ cup firmly packed brown sugar

1 tablespoon butter

1 teaspoon vanilla extract

Powdered sugar

For the batter:
Combine flour, water, baking powder, egg, and cinnamon, adding more water or flour if necessary to make a smooth batter, then set aside for 30 minutes.

❯ Pour oil in a saucepan to about 1 inch deep, then heat over medium-high. Dip the banana pieces in the batter, then fry until golden brown. Remove the bananas from the oil and drain on paper towels.
❯ Meanwhile, in a saucepan, thoroughly combine remaining ingredients except powdered sugar. Cook over medium heat, stirring often, until the sugar has dissolved.
❯ Place banana pieces on serving plates, then thoroughly cover with cream-sugar mixture. Sprinkle with powdered sugar, then serve hot.

CHAPTER 4
Malaysian Cooking
AN ORIENTAL WORLD OF CULINARY DELIGHTS

Kuala Lumpur, Malaysia's capital, is blessed with architectural splendor and a diverse mix of multi-ethnic cultures. The city is saturated with Moorish arches and exquisite minarets seemingly out of the Arabian Nights. Amid this oriental atmosphere, the friendly and hospitable Malaysian Muslims, Chinese Buddhists, Indian Hindus, and Sarawak and Sabah tribal peoples of Malaysia's eastern provinces all work, play, and dine together. Each of these groups has imparted its culinary traditions.

From time immemorial, the tropical, lush-green Malaysia has been a trading center where the peoples of Southeast Asia, the Indian subcontinent, the Arab world, and, later, Europe, settled or met to trade. All who came left traces of their food heritage. Borrowing and adapting from each other's cooking techniques and ingredients, they developed a rich and spicy Malaysian kitchen.

A twin of the Indonesian cuisine, which has a similar history, Malaysian cuisine consists of many exotic and tasty dishes, a tribute to the conglomeration of people who developed the colorful, healthy, and satisfying fare. Today, a culinary journey through this East Asian land is an experience rarely matched in the world of dining.

Being a Muslim country, pork is not found on the menu except in the Chinese community. Chicken, fish, and, to a lesser extent, beef and lamb are cooked with rice and vegetables in innumerable ways. Basil, cardamom, chile peppers, cinnamon, cloves, coriander (both the seeds and the leaves, which are known as cilantro), coconuts, cumin, ginger, lemongrass, lemon and lime juice, mint, nutmeg, pepper, tamarind, and turmeric are the major condiments used to make these dishes moderately spicy and rich in flavors.

As in almost all of Asia, rice (nasi), followed by noodles (mee), are the country's staples.

Often cooked with coconut milk, steamed white rice accompanies every meal. It is so significant to the Malaysian diet that it is almost synonymous with food.

Fish is also very important in the Malaysian kitchen. Broiled, fried, roasted, or used as an ingredient in soups and stews, the country's fruit of the sea is an unforgettable culinary experience.

Satay, a dish common in both Malaysia and Indonesia, is considered to be the king of the country's food. Introduced by Muslim merchants, it is an adaptation of Indian kebabs, with kebabs themselves being of Arab origin.

The aroma of meat roasting over a charcoal fire is a symbol of Malaysia. Served at roadside stands and in luxurious hotels, marinated cubes of chicken or beef, grilled on skewers, are eaten as appetizers, snacks, or a main course, with a peanut sauce, sliced onion and cucumber, and rice cakes.

A Malaysian meal, besides the usual rice and condiments, consists of four to five main dishes served in large central bowls or platters. Diners are given their own plates, soup bowls, forks, and spoons. The fork is used to push food onto the spoon, and the soup and main course are eaten together, the soup serving as the beverage.

Fruits usually follow the main course, and there is a great variety. In addition to the well-known bananas, mangos, oranges, and papayas, there are exotic durian, mangosteen, rambutan, and star fruit. Malaysian desserts, delicate in texture and smooth and rich in taste, are mainly served as snacks.

Visitors who are lucky enough to dine for a few weeks on Malaysian foods will rarely forget this gastronomic experience. However, armchair travelers can also get into the act by trying these few simple recipes. As the Malaysians say, "Selamat mekan!" (Bon appétit!)

Kuak Kacang — Peanut Sauce

Makes about 1 to 1½ cups

4 tablespoons cooking oil
1 medium onion, chopped
6 garlic cloves, chopped
1 fresh hot pepper, seeded and chopped
½ cup ground peanuts or peanut butter
1 tablespoon tamarind paste
1 tablespoon shrimp paste
1 tablespoon firmly packed brown sugar
¼ teaspoon salt
¼ teaspoon ground fennel seeds
¼ teaspoon ground cumin
½ cup water

› *Heat oil in a frying pan, then sauté onion, garlic, and hot pepper for 10 minutes over medium heat. Allow to cool.*
› *Transfer frying pan contents to a food processor. Add remaining ingredients, then process into a thin paste. Add more water if necessary. Use immediately or store in a tightly covered jar and refrigerate. Use within a week.*

Laksa Penang — Fish Soup

Serves about 8

1½ pounds fish fillet, cut into large pieces
6 cups water
1 large onion, chopped
1 small fresh hot pepper, seeded and finely chopped
4 garlic cloves, crushed
2 tablespoons shrimp paste
2 tablespoons tamarind paste
1 tablespoon grated fresh ginger
2 teaspoons salt
½ pound thin noodles, prepared according to package instructions
4 tablespoons shredded cucumber
4 tablespoons shredded lettuce
2 tablespoons finely chopped fresh cilantro
2 tablespoons finely chopped green onion

› *Place fish and water in a saucepan and bring to boil. Cover and cook over medium heat for 30 minutes. Remove fish with a slotted spoon, reserving the water in the saucepan. Shred fish and return to saucepan. Set aside.*
› *Place onion, hot pepper, garlic, shrimp paste, tamarind paste, ginger, and salt in a blender and blend into paste. Add paste to saucepan contents. Bring to boil, then cover and cook over medium heat for 8 minutes.*
› *Place noodles in a large bowl. Pour the saucepan contents over the noodles. Sprinkle with the remaining ingredients and serve immediately.*

Note: *Twice the amount of lemon or tomato paste may be substituted for the tamarind.*

Malaysian Tea

Serves 8

8 cups boiling water
4 bags green tea or 8 teaspoons loose green tea leaves
½ teaspoon cinnamon
¼ teaspoon ground cardamom
2 tablespoons sugar
Flaked almonds (optional)

Place all the ingredients in a teapot and let steep for 2 minutes or to taste. Serve alone or with flaked almonds.

Banana Delight

Serves about 8

8 medium ripe bananas, peeled and sliced into thick rounds
½ cup firmly packed brown sugar
4 tablespoons lemon juice
3 tablespoons butter
1 teaspoon finely grated fresh ginger
¼ teaspoon cinnamon
⅛ teaspoon ground cloves
2 tablespoons shredded coconut

❯ *Preheat oven to 350° F.*
❯ *Place bananas in an 8-inch round baking dish and set aside.*
❯ *Thoroughly mix remaining ingredients except coconut. Spread mixture evenly over the bananas. Bake uncovered for 15 minutes. Sprinkle coconut over top and bake for a further 5 minutes. Serve hot.*

Nasi Kunyit — Steamed Rice

Serves about 8

2 cups long-grain white rice
1 teaspoon turmeric
1 teaspoon salt
4 cups water
½ cup coconut milk

❯ *Place rice, turmeric, salt, and water in a bowl and allow to stand overnight.*
❯ *Drain and place in the top half of a double boiler. Fill bottom half about three-quarters full with water and bring to boil. Set top with rice firmly in place, then steam over medium heat for about 1 hour, stirring a few times. Stir in coconut milk and steam for another 10 minutes. Serve with all types of meat or vegetable dishes or as part of other recipes.*

Malaysian Stir-Fried Cabbage

Serves 6 to 8

4 tablespoons cooking oil

¼ pound beef, cut into very small pieces

½ pound cooked shrimp

1 large onion, finely chopped

1 small fresh hot pepper, seeded and finely chopped

1 small cabbage (about 1½ pounds), shredded

1½ teaspoons salt

½ teaspoon black pepper

Heat oil in a saucepan, then stir-fry beef over medium heat for 5 minutes. Add shrimp, onion, and hot pepper, then stir-fry for a further 10 minutes. Add cabbage, salt, and pepper. Stir-fry until cabbage wilts but remains somewhat crisp. Serve hot.

Sayur Goreng
Stir-Fried Vegetables

Serves about 8

4 tablespoons cooking oil

1 medium onion, finely chopped

1 small fresh hot pepper, seeded and finely chopped

4 garlic cloves, crushed

3 cups shredded cabbage

2 cups shredded carrots

1 cup thinly sliced zucchini

1 large sweet pepper, seeded, quartered, and thinly sliced

1 (12-ounce) can baby corn, drained

2 tablespoons tomato paste

2 tablespoons soy sauce

1 teaspoon salt

½ teaspoon black pepper

4 tablespoons shredded lettuce

1 medium tomato, quartered and thinly sliced

Heat oil over medium-high heat, then sauté onion, hot pepper, and garlic for 5 minutes. Add cabbage, carrots, zucchini, pepper, and corn. Stir-fry for another 5 minutes. Thoroughly stir in tomato paste, soy sauce, salt, and pepper. Spoon vegetables onto a platter. Decorate with lettuce and tomato, then serve hot.

Nasi Goreng
Malaysian Chicken Fried Rice

Serves about 6

4 tablespoons cooking oil

½ pound boneless chicken, cut into ½-inch cubes

1 medium onion, finely chopped

2 garlic cloves, crushed

½ pound cooked shrimp

1 cup fresh or frozen green peas

½ teaspoon salt

½ teaspoon black pepper

⅛ teaspoon cayenne pepper

2 cups cooked medium- or long-grain white rice

6 eggs

4 tablespoons shredded lettuce leaves

A handful of fresh cilantro

½ small tomato, quartered and thinly sliced

❯ Heat oil in saucepan and sauté chicken over medium heat for 5 minutes. Add onion and garlic, then sauté for a further 8 minutes. Stir in shrimp, green peas, salt, pepper, and cayenne pepper, then stir-fry for another 5 minutes. Stir in rice and stir-fry for a few minutes, then place on a platter.
❯ Fry eggs over easy, then place evenly on top. Garnish with lettuce, cilantro, and tomato, then serve as is or with peanut sauce.

Chicken Satay

Serves 6 to 8

½ small onion, chopped

4 garlic cloves, chopped

1 tablespoon soy sauce

2 tablespoons lemon juice

2 tablespoons peanut or olive oil

1 teaspoon ground fennel seeds

½ teaspoon salt

⅛ teaspoon cayenne pepper

2 pounds boneless chicken, cut into 1-inch squares about ½ inch thick

❯ Place all the ingredients, except chicken, in a blender and blend into a thin paste.
❯ Place chicken in a bowl and pour in paste from blender. Stir until chicken pieces are coated, then marinate for 2 hours, stirring occasionally. Place on skewers and barbecue to taste, basting with juice from the bowl.
❯ Serve hot with cooked rice, peanut sauce, cubed raw onions, cubed boiled potatoes, and sliced cucumbers.

Otak-Otak — Fish Paste

Serves 6 to 8

1 pound fish fillet, cut into large pieces

2 eggs

1 large onion, chopped

1 small fresh hot pepper, seeded and chopped

4 garlic cloves, crushed

1 tablespoon tamarind paste

1 tablespoon grated fresh ginger

1 tablespoon ground almonds

1½ teaspoons grated lemon peel

1 teaspoon salt

¼ teaspoon black pepper

¼ teaspoon turmeric

1 cup coconut milk

> Preheat oven to 350° F.
> Place all ingredients in a food processor and process into a paste. Transfer to a baking dish. Cover and bake for 50 minutes. Serve hot from the baking dish or allow to cool and use as a sandwich spread.

Note: In Malaysia, macadamia nuts or filberts are used instead of almonds, and lemongrass instead of lemon peel.

Chicken Rendang

Serves 6 to 8

4 tablespoons cooking oil

2 pounds boneless chicken, cut into small squares

4 garlic cloves, crushed

1 small fresh hot pepper, seeded and finely chopped

1 tablespoon grated fresh ginger

1 teaspoon ground cumin

1 teaspoon ground coriander seeds

1 teaspoon salt

1 teaspoon black pepper

2 cups coconut milk

4 tablespoons finely ground peanuts

2 tablespoons lemon juice

Heat oil in a saucepan and stir-fry chicken on high heat for about 3 minutes. Reduce heat to medium, then add garlic, hot pepper, ginger, cumin, coriander, salt, and pepper and stir-fry for 1 minute. Stir in coconut milk, then cover and simmer over low heat for 45 minutes, stirring occasionally. Stir in peanuts and lemon juice and simmer for a further 5 minutes. Serve hot with sliced pineapple and cooked rice.

CHAPTER 5

The Food of Thailand

FAST BECOMING WORLD-RENOWNED

A blend of Chinese and Indian cuisines, the food of Thailand is unique among the cuisines of Southeast Asia. In the past few decades, this country's delectable dishes have spread across the globe at a speed unprecedented by the culinary arts of any other nation. Thai food has captured the world's palates with its rich variety, intense flavors, fragrant aromas, succulent, spicy taste, and appealing presentation.

Today, the cuisine of Thailand, distinct in its own right and widely recognized as one of the world's finest, can be found in almost every corner of North America and in any part of Europe. According to some surveys, more than a quarter of North Americans are familiar with Thai food, and those who try it are usually ensnared by this Far Eastern cuisine.

The Thai kitchen, which has the quality and consistency of Chinese food and the spiciness of Mexican cuisine, originated in the Guangsi-Gueizhou region of southwestern China, the original homeland of the Thai people. This regional Chinese kitchen was later enriched by the foods brought in by foreign traders and the wealth of tropical fruits and vegetables, fish, herbs, and spices found in the country. The Thais have been able to absorb foreign influences and evolve these into something uniquely their own.

Indian cuisine's aromatic curries, coriander, cumin, red chiles, and turmeric has left an indelible mark on the kitchen of Thailand, as has, to a lesser extent, Portuguese, Dutch, French, and Japanese foods. The country's culinary art is today a combination of Eastern and Western foods, harmoniously combined. The skill of blending five flavors—bitter, hot, salty, sweet, and sour—is the trademark of Thai food.

Generally, Thai food can range from mild to fiery hot and spicy, bursting with unique flavors and appetizing aromas. Some of the ingredients that enhance the country's cuisine include anise, basil, coconuts and their milk, fresh cilantro, curries, galangal, garlic, ginger, lemongrass, lime juice, mango, onions, salted cabbage, palm sugar, tamarind, eggs, soybeans, fish, oyster sauce, and soy sauce. The ideal Thai meal is a homogeneous blend of spices, producing a subtly sweet and sour taste. The dishes are always meant to be equally satisfying to the eye, nose, and mouth.

A Thai meal usually consists of a number of dishes and condiments served with rice as the centerpiece. The dishes complement each other in flavor and texture. Bitter, piquant, and sharp foods are tempered by sweets such as coconut milk and palm sugar. The nuttiness of nuts and the saltiness of some sauces are balanced by zesty fish condiments; the hot peppers are tempered by lime juice; tamarind is balanced by lemongrass.

A typical Thai meal includes a soup, rice or noodles, a steamed dish, a fried dish, a hot salad, and a variety of sauces into which food is dipped. Steaming, frying, and stir-frying are the main cooking methods. All the dishes are served at once, and diners can sample each dish against a background of rice, combining or tasting separately. Rice is an essential ingredient in most Thai meals, and the side dishes act as condiments for this staple of Asia.

Meats and vegetables are served in bite-size

chunks; hence, only a spoon and fork are used when dining. Sometimes a whole meal based on rice or noodles with meat and vegetables is served in a single bowl along with condiments and sauces. Typically, all meals end with elaborate, sweet desserts or a variety of fresh-cut fruit.

Thai salads such as som tam and yam som oh, with a combination of sweet, sour, and spicy dressings, are pungent, hot, and crispy. Soups such as tom yum koong (hot and spicy shrimp soup) and tom kha (coconut herb soup), with their meat, vegetable, and rice or noodle components, often serve as an entire meal. Lunches are usually a one-dish meal. Seasoning sauces and pastes such as nam pla (salted fermented fish sauce), nam prik num (a chile and eggplant-based sauce), kapi (fermented shrimp paste), and ingredients such as dried prawns are characteristic of Thai cooking.

For main courses, chicken, beef, pork, and shrimp—the most common seafood—are used alone or in combination with other meats. Vegetarian dishes such as pad paak ruamit (stir-fried vegetables), bean curd, and tofu are great substitutes for the meats. From the huge Thai kitchen some of the most common main dishes are eggplant with tofu, nue gra pao (stir-fried beef), gai pad khing (ginger chicken), thot man pla (fried fish cakes), and kraphong khao priao wan (sweet and sour fish).

A good number of Thai desserts feature bananas, such as kluay cap (fried bananas), llai buad chi (bananas in coconut milk), and kluay ping (grilled bananas soaked in syrup). Competing with bananas are coconut-based desserts, including sangkha-yaa ma-phrao (coconut custard) and ta-koh (Thai jelly with coconut cream). Many of the Thai desserts are enhanced by the delicate taste of coconut milk and flavored with aromatic pandan leaves and jasmine flowers.

The aromas coming out of the Thai kitchen convey not only flavor but also freshness. However, garnishing the food is what completes its culinary appeal. Attractive presentation is as important as exquisite flavor. Roasted peanuts, bean sprouts, chile peppers, fresh cilantro, and sculptured fruits and shallots, used as garnishes, provide the dishes with a visual definition of the beauty of Thai food.

Thai dishes are not difficult to prepare, but some of the ingredients may be hard to find in some Western countries. For this reason, some internationally accessible ingredients, provided in a number of the recipes below, can replace the original ingredients. Also, the recipes have been simplified so that non-Thai cooks will become familiar with the delightful culinary world of Thailand.

Klai Buad Chi
Bananas in Coconut Milk

Serves 4

3 cups coconut milk

4 tablespoons sugar

¼ teaspoon salt

4 large bananas, sliced in half lengthwise, then cut into 1-inch pieces

Cinnamon (optional)

Place coconut milk, sugar, and salt in a saucepan, then heat over medium-low and stir until sugar dissolves and milk begins to bubble. Gently fold in bananas, then cover and cook over medium heat for 5 minutes without stirring. Place saucepan contents in 4 serving bowls. Sprinkle with cinnamon (optional) and serve.

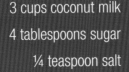

Thai Peanut Sauce

Makes about 1 to 1½ cups

¼ pound roasted peanuts, finely ground

¾ cup coconut milk

½ cup finely chopped fresh cilantro

4 garlic cloves, chopped

2 tablespoons finely chopped onion

1 tablespoon red curry paste

2 teaspoons fish sauce

1 tablespoon grated fresh ginger

4 tablespoons lemon juice

1 tablespoon soy sauce

2 teaspoons sugar

Place all ingredients in a food processor, then process into a smooth sauce. Serve immediately or store in a jar in the refrigerator for a few days.

This peanut sauce can be served with various types of meats and vegetables.

Som Tam — Shrimp Salad

Serves about 6

1 small green papaya (about 1½ pounds), shredded

2 medium tomatoes, diced into 1-inch cubes

½ cup (½-inch pieces) fresh trimmed green beans

¼ cup peanuts, coarsely ground

2 tablespoons fish sauce

1 tablespoon sugar

2 tablespoons finely chopped lemongrass

2 tablespoons lemon juice

2 tablespoons dried shrimp

2 tablespoons seeded and finely chopped fresh chile pepper

4 garlic cloves, crushed

Cabbage leaves

> *Place papaya, tomatoes, beans, and peanuts in a mixing bowl, then set aside.*
> *Use mortar and pestle to crush remaining ingredients, except cabbage leaves. Stir mortar contents into papaya mix, then mix the salad well. Arrange cabbage leaves on a serving dish, then spread salad on top and serve.*

Tom Yum Koong
Shrimp Soup

Serves 6 to 8

5 cups water

½ cup finely chopped green onion

4 tablespoons finely chopped lemongrass

4 garlic cloves, crushed

2 tablespoons fish sauce

2 tablespoons grated fresh ginger

1 fresh large chile pepper, seeded and finely chopped

½ pound fresh shrimp, peeled and deveined

½ pound small mushrooms, thoroughly washed and halved

1 teaspoon salt

3 tablespoons lemon juice

2 teaspoons white sugar

4 tablespoons finely chopped fresh cilantro

Place water, green onion, lemongrass, garlic, fish sauce, ginger, and chile in a saucepan, then bring to boil. Cover and cook over medium heat for 5 minutes, then add shrimp and mushrooms. Cook until the shrimp turn pink, then add salt, lemon juice, and sugar. Cook for 1 minute, then remove from the heat. Stir in cilantro, then serve hot.

Eggplant with Tofu

Serves about 4

½ pound extra firm tofu, diced into ½-inch cubes

¾ cup vegetable oil

4 garlic cloves, crushed

1 medium eggplant, cut into thin slices ½ inch thick and 2 inches long

2 tablespoons finely chopped fresh cilantro

1 tablespoon seeded and finely chopped fresh chile pepper

2 tablespoons chopped fresh basil leaves

2 tablespoons yellow bean sauce

› *Deep-fry tofu in ¼ cup of oil over medium to medium-high heat until golden on all sides. Drain on paper towels.*
› *In a frying pan, heat remaining ½ cup oil over medium-low, then add garlic, eggplant, cilantro, and chile pepper. Stir-fry over high heat for 3 minutes or until eggplant is done. Gently stir in tofu and remaining ingredients, then stir-fry for 2 minutes. Serve immediately.*

Nue Gra Pao
Stir-Fried Beef

Serves about 6

1 tablespoon seeded and finely chopped fresh chile pepper

1 medium onion, chopped

5 garlic cloves, crushed

4 tablespoons vegetable oil

1 pound tender steak, cut into thin strips about ¼ inch thick and 2 inches long

2 tablespoons fish sauce

1 tablespoon sugar

1 teaspoon dried thyme

¾ cup water

½ cup finely chopped fresh mint leaves

Lettuce leaves

> *Place chile, onion, garlic, and 3 tablespoons of oil in a blender, then blend for 1 minute and set aside.*

> *Heat remaining oil in frying pan or wok, then add blender contents and stir-fry for 1 minute. Add meat, then stir-fry until light brown. Stir in fish sauce, sugar, thyme, water, and mint, adding more water if necessary to make about a ½ cup of sauce, then stir-fry for 1 minute. Arrange lettuce leaves in a shallow bowl, then spread mixture over top and serve hot.*

Gai Pad Khing
Ginger Chicken

Serves about 6

Sauce:

2 tablespoons oyster sauce

1 tablespoon fish sauce

1 tablespoon soy sauce

4 tablespoons vegetable oil

1 pound boneless chicken breast, cut into ½-inch cubes

5 garlic cloves, crushed

4 tablespoons grated fresh ginger

2 cups mushrooms, sliced

1 sweet red pepper, seeded and thinly sliced

1 medium onion, thinly sliced

2 tablespoons seeded and finely chopped fresh red chile pepper

2 tablespoons finely chopped green onion

1 tablespoon sugar

Fresh cilantro

For the sauce:

> *Mix oyster, fish, and soy sauces, then set aside.*

> *Heat oil over high heat in a wok or frying pan, then stir-fry chicken, garlic, and ginger for 1 minute.*

> *Add the sauce mix, then stir-fry for 2 minutes. Stir in remaining ingredients, except cilantro. Stir-fry until the chicken is cooked. Place on serving platter, garnish with cilantro, and serve piping hot.*

Thot Man Pla
Fried Fish Patties

Serves about 4

1 pound fish fillet, cut into pieces

2 eggs, beaten

4 tablespoons finely chopped green onion

4 garlic cloves, crushed

4 tablespoons finely chopped lemongrass

2 tablespoons finely chopped fresh cilantro

1 tablespoon grated fresh ginger

½ teaspoon black pepper

½ teaspoon grated lemon rind

1 tablespoon shrimp paste

2 tablespoons finely ground dried chile pepper

1 cup finely chopped green beans

Vegetable oil

❯ *Place all ingredients, except beans and vegetable oil, in a food processor. Process until ingredients become a fine paste. Transfer to a mixing bowl, then combine with the beans. Form into small patties, then set aside. If paste is too soft, add a little flour.*
❯ *Pour oil to about 2 inches deep in a saucepan, then heat. Deep-fry the fish patties until golden brown. Serve with* Thai Peanut Sauce *(see page 64) or another sharp-tasting sauce.*

Kraphong Khao Priao Wan
Sweet and Sour Fish

Serves about 6

1 tablespoon cornstarch

2 tablespoons soy sauce

1 teaspoon garlic powder

½ teaspoon black pepper

1 pound fish fillet, cut into 2-square-inch pieces

4 tablespoons vegetable oil

1 large onion, thinly sliced

1 tablespoon seeded and finely chopped fresh chile pepper

4 tomatoes, diced into ½-inch cubes

1 tablespoon ketchup

1 tablespoon white vinegar

1 tablespoon fish sauce

1 tablespoon sugar

½ cup (½-inch cubed) fresh pineapple

❯ *Combine cornstarch, soy sauce, garlic powder, and pepper, then coat fish pieces with this mixture and set aside for 1 hour.*
❯ *Heat oil in a frying pan or wok, then fry fish on high heat for about 4 minutes or until fish pieces turn light brown, turning them over a few times. Remove and set aside.*
❯ *In the same oil, adding more if necessary, stir-fry onion and chile pepper until limp. Add tomatoes and stir-fry for 1 minute, then add fish and remaining ingredients except pineapple. Gently stir-fry for 2 minutes, then stir in pineapple and serve.*

Pad Paak Ruamit
Stir-Fried Vegetables

Serves about 6

4 tablespoons peanut oil

½ pound broccoli, chopped

1 pound fresh or thawed frozen corn

½ pound spinach leaves, thoroughly washed and chopped

¼ pound mushrooms, sliced

2 tablespoons seeded and finely chopped chile pepper

1 medium onion, thinly sliced

4 garlic cloves, crushed

4 tablespoons finely chopped lemongrass

2 tablespoons fish or oyster sauce

1 tablespoon soy sauce

1 tablespoon sugar

1 cup bean sprouts

Heat oil in a wok or frying pan, then add all ingredients except sugar and bean sprouts. Stir-fry vegetables for 4 minutes, then stir in sugar and bean sprouts and serve immediately.

Thai-Style Cooked Rice

Serves about 8

3 tablespoons vegetable oil

1 medium onion, finely chopped

4 garlic cloves, crushed

1 tablespoon grated fresh ginger

1½ cups long-grain white rice, rinsed

½ cup coconut milk

½ cup fresh or frozen green peas

2¼ cups water

½ teaspoon salt

Heat oil in a large saucepan, then add onion, garlic, and ginger. Stir-fry over medium-high heat for 5 minutes. Add rice and stir-fry for 1 minute. Add remaining ingredients, then bring to boil. Stir and cover, then reduce heat to low. Cook for 20 minutes, stirring a number of times to ensure that rice does not stick to bottom of pan, then re-cover. Turn off heat and let sit covered for 20 minutes. Fluff with fork and serve.

CHAPTER 6

The Delectable Foods of Vietnam

While Vietnamese food has long been appreciated in France, Vietnam's former colonial master, other people in the Western Hemisphere are only beginning to discover its many healthy yet exotically tasty attributes. Its reliance on rice, wheat, raw or semi-raw vegetables, and all types of fresh herbs, with a scant use of meats and oil, makes it an ideal cuisine for the health-conscious. Some food writers claim that the Vietnamese possess a culinary kitchen that is among the healthiest on the globe.

As is true of many other facets of life in Vietnam, a nation of 70 million, the food of the country is saturated with Chinese influences. Once under the colonial rule of China, the Vietnamese took on chopsticks and the wok, in addition to Buddhism and Confucianism. Their kitchen was a spillover of Chinese cuisine, with a touch of the culinary arts adopted from other neighboring countries. However, in the last century the French have heavily influenced Vietnamese cuisine. Even though rice remains the staple, the French baguette is much favored. These influences, and the bountiful ingredients found in the countryside, make food a daily glorification of life.

From the centuries of foreign domination, and because of its great northern and southern fertile rice baskets—the Red River and Mekong deltas—Vietnamese food developed its own character. Soy sauce is rarely used. Instead, nuoc mam fish sauce, the most important ingredient in all of Vietnamese cuisine and the base of all its piquant dips, replaces many condiments and seasonings in cooking. It is almost always served with Vietnamese meals, just as we serve salt and pepper.

As to the cooking process, unlike the Chinese, stir-frying plays only a small role in the kitchen of Vietnam. Simmering the food is the usual method of cooking.

Vietnam's culinary delights vary greatly from the north to the south. However, all have noodles as their main base, or rice. The Vietnamese are noodle fanatics. At home, in restaurants, or standing at food stands, they consume noodles in great quantities for the three meals of the day. Made from mung beans, rice, or wheat, noodles are eaten in soups and entrées, and fried crisp with the meal or eaten for snacks.

Fresh vegetables and herbs are also always served. No meal is complete without a plate of freshly sliced cucumbers, hot peppers, and bean sprouts, with sprigs of basil, cilantro, mint, or other related herbs.

There are some important differences in the regional cuisines. The northern Vietnamese have a fondness for beef and use much more black pepper than chiles; the dishes are not as rich or spicy as the foods of the country's south. The food is hottest in central Vietnam. Hot peppers overflow in the marketplaces, and cooks use them with great ingenuity to enhance their dishes. Farther south, in the areas surrounding Saigon, the cook's trademark is fresh vegetables. Here the cuisine has taken much from the French kitchen, including the baguette whose aroma entices the passersby in the early morning hours.

A number of dishes are common throughout the country. Cha ca *(fish balls)*, cha gio or nem ran *(spring rolls of meat and vegetables)*, gio lua *(a type of sausage)*, and pho bo *(beef noodle soup)* are served from Hanoi in the north to Saigon in the south. Worldwide, pho bo *is the best known of all Vietnamese soup dishes. Eaten as a snack, with a meal, or often for breakfast, it consists of a broth with rice noodles and beef or chicken, fresh herbs, and onion, often with the addition of lime juice, chile peppers, and vinegar. It is usually accompanied with* quay *(fried dough).*

Overshadowing these popular foods are the seafood dishes. Crab, lobster, mussels, shrimp, squid, and countless types of fish are typical daily foods in all Vietnamese households or restaurants. Also, without exception, soups are popular, almost always consumed at every meal.

From men ga *(a chicken and fish sauce noodle soup, spiced with herbs) and* hu tieu *(a chicken, meat, and shrimp soup served with a broth over rice noodles) to* canh chua *(a seafood sweet and sour soup served with fruit and green herbs) and* mang tay nau cua *(an asparagus and crab meat soup), soups entice the taste buds—all mouth-watering either as single meals or side dishes.*

The meals are usually served with long-grain rice, nuoc mam, *and a wide range of fresh herbs and vegetables. Generally, chopsticks are used. However, if European food is served, it is eaten with a fork and knife, especially when there are foreign guests.*

The following are my own versions of typical Vietnamese dishes. I have substituted some ingredients not easily found in North America. However, they are still mainly the same as those traditionally prepared.

Vietnamese Sweet and Sour Tofu

Serves about 8

4 tablespoons lemon juice
4 tablespoons *Nuoc Mam* (see "Asian Condiments" section)
4 tablespoons water
4 tablespoons tomato paste
2 tablespoons sugar
1 teaspoon ground ginger
4 garlic cloves, crushed
1 pound extra firm tofu, drained and diced into ½-inch cubes
3 tablespoons vegetable oil
1 cup chopped green onion
2 medium sweet peppers, seeded and sliced in thin strips
1 pound mushrooms, sliced
1 cup toasted cashews

> *Combine well lemon juice, Nuoc Mam, water, tomato paste, sugar, ginger, and garlic, then gently stir in tofu and allow to marinate overnight.*
> *Heat oil in frying pan, then stir-fry green onion, sweet peppers, and mushrooms for 3 minutes over medium-high heat. Stir in the tofu mixture with its marinade, then continue to stir-fry for 4 minutes. Remove from heat, then stir in cashews and serve over cooked rice.*

Nuoc Cham — Hot Fish Sauce

Makes about 1 cup

4 fresh medium red chile peppers, seeded and chopped

4 garlic cloves, crushed

1 tablespoon grated fresh ginger

1 tablespoon sugar

1 tablespoon water

2 tablespoons lime or lemon juice

2 tablespoons white vinegar

3 tablespoons *Nuoc Mam* (see "Asian Condiments" section)

4 tablespoons finely chopped fresh cilantro

Place all ingredients in a food processor and process for 1 minute, then serve with all types of entrées or soups.

Mang Tay Nau Cua
Asparagus and Crab Meat Soup

Serves 8

2 tablespoons peanut oil

½ cup finely chopped green onion

4 garlic cloves, crushed

½ pound fresh or frozen crab meat, cut into small pieces

2 tablespoons *Nuoc Mam* (see "Asian Condiments" section)

½ teaspoon black pepper

5 cups chicken broth

1 teaspoon sugar

2 tablespoons cornstarch, diluted in ¼ cup water

2 eggs, beaten

2 cups chopped fresh asparagus

2 tablespoons finely chopped fresh cilantro

2 tablespoons finely chopped fresh basil

Heat oil in a frying pan. Add green onion and garlic and stir-fry over medium heat for 3 minutes. Add crab meat, 1 tablespoon of the Nuoc Mam, and pepper, then stir-fry over high heat for 1 minute and set aside. Place remaining 1 tablespoon of the Nuoc Mam, broth, and sugar in a saucepan, then bring to a boil. Stir in diluted cornstarch. Reduce to medium heat and gently stir until the soup begins to thicken. Stir in the eggs and continue to gently stir for a further 1 minute. Stir in the crab meat mixture and asparagus and bring to boil. Cook for 5 minutes, stirring a few times. Transfer to a serving bowl. Sprinkle with cilantro and basil just before serving.

Cha Gio or *Nem Ran* — Spring Rolls of Meat and Vegetables

Makes 30 rolls

Marinade:

3 tablespoons *Nuoc Cham* (see page 51)

3 tablespoons water

⅛ teaspoon cayenne pepper

1 tablespoon sesame oil

1 tablespoon cornstarch

½ pound chicken breast, cut into thin strips about 1 inch long

2 ounces thin rice noodles, broken up

2 tablespoons peanut oil

1 tablespoon grated fresh ginger

1 small onion, finely chopped

4 garlic cloves, crushed

1 small sweet red pepper, seeded and sliced into thin strips about 1 inch long

1 cup mushrooms, sliced

½ cup finely chopped green onion

2 tablespoons finely chopped fresh cilantro

Rice paper rounds about 8 inches in diameter

Oil for deep-frying

To make marinade:

❯ *Combine* Nuoc Cham, *water, cayenne pepper, and sesame oil, then stir in cornstarch.*

❯ *Add chicken, then stir to coat. Marinate for 30 minutes.*

❯ *While the chicken is marinating, cook noodles for 5 minutes in boiling water. Drain and set aside.*

❯ *In frying pan, heat peanut oil. Add ginger, onion, and garlic and stir-fry over medium-high heat for 30 seconds. Add red pepper and mushrooms, then stir-fry for 2 minutes. Add chicken with its marinade and stir-fry for a further 4 minutes. Stir in noodles, green onion, and cilantro, then allow to cool.*

❯ *Soften rice paper by dipping papers, one at a time, into warm water. Place about 1 heaping tablespoon of filling in center of each sheet, then fold the bottom over the filling. Fold each side over the center and roll up tightly.*

❯ *In a saucepan, heat oil, then fry rolls over medium-high heat for about 4 minutes or until golden on all sides.*

Note: *Instead of frying, rolls can be baked for 25 minutes in an oven preheated to 350° F, then browned under the broiler. Serve hot with* Nuoc Cham *or* Sot Ca Chua *sauce (see pages 51 and 55).*

Cha Ca — Fish and Noodles

Serves 4

½ pound thin noodles

2 tablespoons *Nuoc Mam* (see "Asian Condiments" section)

½ teaspoon turmeric

2 teaspoons ground ginger

2 teaspoons garlic powder

½ teaspoon black pepper

2 tablespoons vegetable oil

1 pound fish fillet, cut into medium-size pieces

1 cup chopped green onion

1 cup chopped fresh dill

½ cup chopped fresh basil

4 tablespoons roasted peanuts, chopped

❯ *Cook noodles according to directions on package, then divide into 4 serving bowls and set aside.*

❯ *In a bowl, combine Nuoc Mam, turmeric, ginger, garlic powder, pepper, and 1 tablespoon of the oil. Add fish and stir until all the pieces are coated. Place in the refrigerator and allow to marinate for 30 minutes.*

❯ *Heat remainder of oil in a wok or heavy frying pan until oil begins to smoke, then stir-fry fish for 2 minutes. Remove from heat, then stir in onion and half the dill.*

❯ *Top noodles in each bowl with fish, then cover with remaining dill and basil. Sprinkle with peanuts and serve immediately with Nuoc Cham (see page 51).*

Ga Xao Xa Ot
Chicken with Lemongrass

Serves 4 to 6

4 tablespoons vegetable oil

2 medium onions, thinly sliced

4 garlic cloves, thinly sliced

2 tablespoons finely chopped lemongrass

1 fresh small chile pepper, seeded and finely chopped

2 pounds boneless chicken breast, cut into ½-inch cubes

½ teaspoon salt

3 tablespoons *Nuoc Mam* (see "Asian Condiments" Section)

1 tablespoon sugar

1½ cups water

In frying pan, heat oil over medium heat. Add onion and garlic, then stir-fry for 3 minutes. Add lemongrass and chile, then stir-fry for a further 2 minutes. Stir in chicken and fry for a further 5 minutes, stirring often. Add remaining ingredients, then cover and allow to simmer over low heat for 40 minutes or until chicken becomes tender, stirring often. Add more water if necessary. Serve hot.

Garlic Lamb

Serves about 6

½ cup fresh cilantro, packed

4 tablespoons vegetable oil

1½ pounds lamb, thinly sliced

1 small head garlic, crushed

3 tablespoons *Nuoc Mam* (see "Asian Condiments" Section)

2 tablespoons oyster sauce

1 tablespoon sugar

1 teaspoon black pepper

1 fresh chile pepper, seeded and finely chopped

❯ *Spread cilantro on a serving platter, then set aside.*

❯ *Heat oil in a wok or heavy frying pan, then stir-fry lamb over medium-high heat for 4 minutes. Stir in remaining ingredients and continually stir-fry until lamb is cooked. Ladle lamb with its sauce over cilantro and serve immediately.*

Try Cai — Fruit in Syrup

Serves 6 to 8

A very light, juicy, and refreshing dessert, the canned lychees called for in this recipe are available at Asian groceries or supermarkets that have international food sections.

4 tablespoons sugar

2 tablespoons water

2 tablespoons pineapple juice

2 tablespoons lemon juice

1 medium orange, sectioned, then sections sliced in half

2 cups (½-inch cubes) fresh pineapple

2 cups canned lychees

1 cup coconut milk

❯ *Place sugar and water in a saucepan, then stir and cook over medium heat for 6 minutes, adding a little water if necessary. Set aside syrup and allow to cool.*

❯ *Place remaining ingredients in a serving bowl, then pour the syrup over the fruit and toss.*

❯ *Chill in refrigerator, then serve.*

Sot Ca Chua
Tomato Sauce

Makes about 1 to 1½ cups

2 tablespoons peanut oil
6 garlic cloves, crushed
4 medium tomatoes, seeded and finely chopped
1 cup coconut milk
⅓ cup water
1 teaspoon salt
1 teaspoon sugar

In a frying pan, heat oil, then stir-fry garlic over high heat for 1 minute. Add tomatoes, then sauté over medium heat for 5 minutes. Stir in remaining ingredients, then bring to boil. Simmer uncovered over medium heat, stirring every few minutes, until sauce thickens, then serve with all types of entrées.

Pho Bo
Beef Noodle Soup

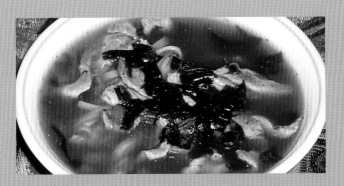

Serves 8

15 cups water
4 pounds beef, lamb, or chicken bones, or a mixture of these
3 medium onions, finely chopped
4 garlic cloves, chopped
4 tablespoons chopped fresh ginger
2 cinnamon sticks, each about 3 inches long
2 teaspoons salt
1 tablespoon sugar
4 whole cloves
1 teaspoon whole black peppercorns
1 pound flat rice noodles
1 pound lean, tender beef, sliced paper thin
Nuoc Mam to taste (see "Asian Condiments" section)
½ cup finely chopped green onion
4 tablespoons finely chopped fresh cilantro
2 cups bean sprouts
8 large sprigs fresh basil
2 fresh large red chile peppers, seeded and thinly sliced
6 limes, halved

This is one of the most popular dishes throughout of Vietnam and in Vietnamese restaurants throughout the world.

❭ *Place in a large saucepan: water, bones, onion, garlic, ginger, cinnamon, salt, sugar, cloves, and peppercorns. Bring to boil. Skim foam a few times, then cook over medium-low heat for 4 hours, adding water to cover the bones. Remove bones and strain out vegetables and seasonings to make a clear broth.*
❭ *In the meantime, cook noodles in boiling water for 8 minutes, then drain and divide into 8 large soup bowls. Place the thinly sliced beef evenly over top of noodles.*
❭ *Season broth with Nuoc Mam and bring to boil, then stir in green onion and cilantro. Pour over meat and noodles, then stir to cook meat. Serve with a large platter of bean sprouts, basil, peppers, and lime so that diners may add these to taste.*

CHAPTER 7
The Japanese Kitchen

A CUISINE OF THE AGES

The creation of Japanese cuisine began about 400 B.C., when rice was first introduced by Chinese migrants who arrived in the country through the Korean peninsula and directly by sea from China. It gradually became the main staple in the country. A short time later, wheat, soy sauce, tea, and chopsticks were introduced into the island kingdom from China. Subsequently, all of these became an important part of Japan's culinary world.

Buddhism was introduced along with these other contributions from Korea and China, and in the sixth century A.D. it became the state religion. Hence, meat was forbidden for a millennium. It was only after the coming of the Portuguese in the sixteenth century that meat was once again found on the daily menu. Tempura, one of today's mainstays of the Japanese kitchen, was introduced by the Portuguese and has become as Japanese as fish and chips is British.

From the snowcapped mountains on northern Hokkaido to the sandy shores of Okinawa, Japan covers a huge territory consisting of thousands of islands. Naturally, there are differences in diet and cooking styles between the various regions of the country. The different products found within each helped in the development of special regional dishes.

The Japanese love to eat their food fresh and in season. The country's traditional culture revolves around the changing seasons, featuring foods such as chestnuts and eggplant in autumn, bamboo shoots and herring in spring, and bonito in summer. Great emphasis is placed on freshness and natural flavor.

For centuries, the basic Japanese staple has been rice with fish. Almost as important are the vegetables that form the nucleus of the side dishes. These are made even tastier by mirin, a sweet saki, as well as miso and shoyu condiments made from fermented soy sauce.

Rice, the short-grain variety, is served with every meal and is, by far, the most important crop in Japan, transformed into a number of essential products. Repeated annually for millennia, various ceremonies are offered to the gods for each of the yearly cycles of sowing, transplanting, and harvesting the crop.

Rice is also used to make paper and wine, as well as fuel, animal food, and building materials. Until the nineteenth century, rice was used as a currency for paying taxes and wages. The amount of rice one had indicated one's economic status in society.

In the Japanese culinary world, sushi is one of the most popular dishes and is fast spreading worldwide. Sushi restaurants have become popular even in North America. For sushi lovers, there is no more appetizing a sight than a conveyer belt carrying plates of sushi round and round for customers to select their choices.

Tempura owes its origin to Portuguese missionaries. It is perhaps better known internationally than sushi. This tasty dish made from chicken, seafood, or vegetables has become a traditional Japanese dish served in gourmet restaurants, as well as from pushcarts and side-walk stalls. Most connoisseurs of this dish agree that fresh ingredients are essential to make a delicious tempura.

In the past half century, Japanese food has spread worldwide. The traditional Japanese dishes, very low in cholesterol, fat, and calories, but high in fiber, have given the Japanese among the highest life spans on the globe. One of the healthiest all-round cuisines to be found in any nation, the food of Japan goes well beyond the well-known raw fish, tempura, and tofu dishes. Teriyaki, grilled fish, meats, or vegetables marinated in a delicious sauce; nabemono, a hearty chicken, seafood, and vegetable wintertime dish; unagi, a grilled eel delicacy; yakitori, grilled chicken and vegetables dipped in barbecue sauce; okonomiyaki, a savory meat and vegetable pancake; oyakodon, a Japanese rice bowl; and oden, a stew made from fish dumplings and a series of other ingredients, are commonly found in everyday meals.

To eat in Japan is a ceremony of harmony. The Japanese say that before eating the food you must enjoy it with the eyes. The people are enamored with the artistic beauty of a displayed arrangement of the food and the utensils.

For a fine meal, the ingredients of one dish must be in harmony together, and that dish must be in harmony with the other dishes. Food must also be in harmony with nature and the surroundings. To eat the traditional way, every meal is an exercise in beauty and tenderness. The more beautiful the food looks, the more delicious the food is thought to be.

The following traditional Japanese dishes that I have re-created will provide a sample of the rich and varied Japanese kitchen. They are perhaps not all in harmony, but they are tasty and simple to prepare. After trying these dishes, I am sure you will say, "Gochiso-sama"—the Japanese expression to give thanks for a fine meal.

Korokke — Potato Patties

Serves 4

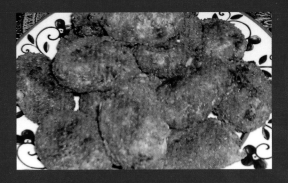

3 tablespoons butter
1 medium onion, finely chopped
½ pound ground beef
3 cups mashed potatoes
1 teaspoon salt
½ teaspoon black pepper
Oil for frying
White flour
2 eggs, beaten
Bread crumbs

❯ Melt butter in frying pan, then sauté onion over medium heat for 8 minutes. Add beef, then stir-fry for a further 5 minutes. Remove and allow to cool.

❯ Add potatoes, salt, and pepper to meat and thoroughly mix. Form into oval-shaped patties.

❯ Pour oil in a saucepan to about 1 inch deep and heat.

❯ Dredge patties in flour, then dip into egg. Coat with bread crumbs, then fry over medium heat until brown. Serve immediately.

Tsukune
Chicken Meatballs

Serves 4 to 6

1 pound ground chicken

½ cup finely chopped mushrooms

½ cup fine bread crumbs

¼ cup finely chopped onions

1 egg, beaten

1 tablespoon finely grated fresh ginger

1 tablespoon *Shoyu* (see "Asian Condiments" section)

1 tablespoon *Mirin* (see "Asian Condiments" section)

½ teaspoon salt

Vegetable oil for frying

Combine well all ingredients except oil. Form mixture into small balls and set aside. Pour oil to about ¾ inch deep in a frying pan, then fry balls over medium heat until they brown. Serve hot.

Miso Vegetable Soup

Serves 6 to 8

1 medium potato, peeled and diced into ½-inch cubes

1 medium carrot, cut into thin ½-inch rounds

2 cups *Dashi* stock (see "Asian Condiments" section)

½ medium head broccoli or ½ small head of cauliflower, broken into florets

1 medium onion, finely chopped

1 cup shredded cabbage

2 teaspoons dried basil

1 teaspoon dried marjoram

2 tablespoons *miso*, dissolved in 4 cups water

In a saucepan place potato, carrot, and stock. Bring to boil. Cover and cook over medium-low heat for 40 minutes. Add remaining ingredients, then re-cover and bring to boil. Cook for a further 10 minutes. Serve immediately.

ASIAN COOKING MADE SIMPLE

Tatsuta
Japanese-Style Fried Chicken

Serves about 6

2 pounds boneless chicken breast, cut into small pieces

4 tablespoons *Shoyu* (see "Asian Condiments" section)

5 tablespoons *Mirin* (see "Asian Condiments" section)

5 tablespoons ginger juice

Oil for frying

¾ cup cornstarch

> *Combine in a small bowl chicken, shoyu, mirin, and ginger juice and allow to marinate for 4 hours, stirring a few times. With a slotted spoon, remove chicken from marinade and pat dry on paper towels.*
> *Pour oil in a saucepan to about ½ inch deep and heat over medium.*
> *Roll chicken pieces in cornstarch, then fry until golden brown. Remove with slotted spoon and drain on paper towels before serving.*

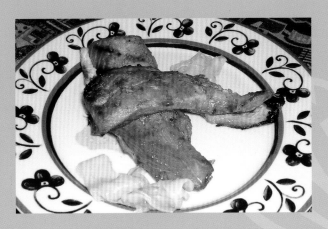

Salmon Teriyaki

Serves 6 to 8

3 pounds salmon fillet, cut into 6 to 8 serving pieces

Marinade:

¾ cup soy sauce

¾ cup firmly packed light brown sugar

¼ cup orange juice

4 tablespoons lemon juice

6 garlic cloves, crushed

1 tablespoon grated fresh ginger

1 teaspoon black pepper

1 teaspoon dry mustard

Place fillets in a baking dish and set aside.

For the marinade:
Make a marinade by combining remaining ingredients. Pour over fillets and allow to marinate for about 5 hours, turning them over a number of times. Remove salmon steaks from marinade and wrap with aluminum foil. Grill salmon, turning over once, for about 10 minutes or until fish flakes when pressed with a fork.

Japanese Cooked Rice

Serves 4 to 6

2 cups short-grain white rice, soaked for 30 minutes and drained

3 cups water

Place rice and water in a saucepan and bring to boil. Reduce heat to low and cover. Cook for 15 minutes, stirring a number of times then re-covering. Stir, then re-cover and turn off heat. Let sit for 30 minutes before serving.

Nigiri Sushi — Tuna Sushi

Makes 20 to 25 sushis

2½ tablespoons *wasabi* paste

1 pound fresh tuna, very thinly sliced

2 cups Japanese Cooked Rice (see above), formed into 16 balls

Spread a very tiny amount of wasabi *paste* on a tuna slice, then place slice in the hand. Place ball of rice on top of tuna slice, then close hand to mold tuna to the rice. Use both hands to flatten slightly and mold into a rectangle. Continue until all the rice balls are finished. Serve with soy sauce, wasabi *paste*, and pickled ginger.

Japanese Peanut Cookies

Makes 25 to 30 cookies

2 cups white flour

½ cup butter, melted

1¼ cups firmly packed brown sugar

2 eggs, beaten

1 teaspoon vanilla extract

½ cup peanut butter

The traditional way to make these cookies is to use peanuts instead of peanut butter.

❯ Preheat oven to 350° F.
❯ Place all ingredients in a mixing bowl, then thoroughly knead, adding a little water if necessary. Form into walnut-size balls, then flatten on cookie sheets into cookie shape.
❯ Bake for 20 minutes. Allow to cool before serving.

Shrimp Tempura

Serves 4 to 6

1 cup white flour

2 tablespoons cornstarch

1 tablespoon baking powder

½ teaspoon salt

1 egg, beaten

1 cup cold water

Vegetable oil

2 pounds uncooked tiger shrimp, peeled and deveined

❯ Combine flour, cornstarch, baking powder, and salt. Stir in egg and water to make a batter and set aside.

❯ Pour oil to about 2 inches deep in a saucepan and heat. Dip shrimp, a few at a time, into batter, then fry over medium heat until golden brown—6 to 8 minutes. Remove with slotted spoon and drain on paper towels.

Dora Yaki
Bean Pancake

Makes about 10 sandwiches

Batter:

2 cups white flour

2 tablespoons sugar

½ teaspoon salt

1 teaspoon baking powder

½ teaspoon baking soda

1 egg, beaten

1½ cups water

Vegetable oil

1 (6-ounce) can azuki beans, drained and mashed with enough honey to make a paste

These pancakes are very popular in Japan. They are also made with other fillings and make excellent snacks. For this recipe, I used azuki (also called aduki) beans that have a sweet and nutty flavor. These beans are available in Asian supermarkets.

For the batter:
Combine flour, sugar, salt, baking powder, and baking soda in a bowl, then stir in egg and water to make a pancake-like batter and set aside.

❯ Heat griddle and swab with oil. Drop about 2 tablespoons of batter on the hot griddle. When it bubbles, flip it over and cook for a further 30 seconds. Continue until all the batter has been used. Spread bean paste on a pancake, then top with another to form a sandwich. Continue for the remainder of the pancakes.

CHAPTER 8

The Korean Kitchen

AN ARRAY OF CULTURES

Korean cuisine belongs to the same family of foods as that of the Chinese and Japanese. However, compared to the Japanese, Koreans rely less on the creatures of the sea; in contrast to the Chinese, they use less oil in their cooking. Similar to both the Chinese and Japanese, however, rice is the main staple, followed by noodles.

Koreans like their food spicier, mostly by the generous use of ginger, and chile—which was introduced by the Portuguese. In fact, the most distinguishing feature of Korean food is its spiciness. Korea is surrounded on three sides by water, and even though the per capita consumption of fish is lower than in Japan, all types of seafood remain the mainstays of the diet. Koreans have eaten the products of the sea for centuries, and their markets today overflow with all types of fish, clams, crabs, octopus, oysters, shrimp, and squid. These are barbecued, broiled, fried, pickled, steamed, stewed, or dried and crushed to make pastes and sauces. Medium-grain rice is even more important than seafood in the Korean diet. Rice is served with all meals. The variety grown in Korea is somewhat different from varieties produced elsewhere. When cooked, it remains moist and becomes sticky, making it easy to eat with chopsticks. Another item that appears with every meal is kimchi, often called "Korea's national dish." It is a fermented and highly seasoned vegetable dish traditionally made from cabbage. Today, this spicy pickled condiment is made from countless varieties of vegetables, herbs, and spices and, at times, seasoned with dried and salted shrimp, anchovies, and oysters. It is said that visitors cannot really say that they have eaten Korean food if they have not tasted kimchi, varieties of which are sold in Korean and other Asian markets.

Besides kimchi, the Koreans use a series of other condiments and sauces to flavor their food, including jang made from fermented soybeans, and gochu jang, a hot, fermented chile paste.

Beef, chicken, and pork are at times mixed together and at other times mixed with fish. When vegetables are added, the outcome is tasty casseroles and appetizing and flavorful stews. Fritters made from a varied mixture of ingredients and cooked on a griddle or pan-fried are also often made at home, or served in restaurants, street carts, or stalls. Other common Korean dishes are ginseng chicken soup in a clay pot; sokkori kuk, an oxtail soup; bibimbap, a mixed vegetable and rice dish; ho-baechu, stir-fried cabbage; kong jang, a black bean potage; mandu, Korean-type dumplings; yak-ka, a chestnut sweet; and gimbap, rice wrapped in seaweed, Korea's most popular and nutritious convenience dish.

The two dishes most in demand by tourists and outsiders are kalbi and pulgogi, both barbecued meat dishes just a little different from each other. They are made from beef or pork and marinated in a sauce that is not too highly spiced.

They are served in restaurants, usually cooked at the customer's table over charcoal fires.

The Koreans are proud of their diet, which is quite varied and nutritious. They use little meat and many grains and vegetables. The dishes contain moderate calories and little fat. The introduction of fast food, and its popularity with the young, could change things in the future.

A Korean family meal has its arrangements and traditions. Usually the family sits on the floor around a low table. On the table are always three essentials for every meal: rice, soup, and kimchi. The number of side dishes (called chops) served with these essentials classifies the table setting. These could be from three to twelve for an ordinary meal, or many more for a feast.

There is no set order in which to eat. Usually soup and rice are served in individual bowls, and diners share the other dishes. There is no particular arrangement of food on the plates and dishes on the table. Foods are usually placed neatly in concentric circles or parallel linear columns and never in a disorderly fashion, with the color of the food alternating in a regular manner. The chopsticks and spoons, unlike those of the Chinese and Japanese, are not made of wood, but of stainless steel and earthenware.

To really know Korean food, it is best to partake in a Korean feast. However, one can enjoy the delights of the Korean kitchen by preparing these few traditional Korean dishes, which I have simplified and re-created to my own taste.

Kalbi — Beef Ribs

Serves 4 to 6

4 pounds crosscut beef short ribs, cut about 1½ inches wide and 1½ inches thick

1 medium onion, finely chopped

4 garlic cloves, crushed

2 tablespoons grated fresh ginger

½ cup finely chopped green onion

1 small fresh hot pepper, seeded and finely chopped

⅓ cup soy sauce

¼ cup Korean malt syrup

1 tablespoon light sesame oil

1 teaspoon black pepper

> Place ribs in cold water for about 2 hours, then drain and pat dry with paper towels. Place in a large bowl.
> Combine the remaining ingredients, then pour over ribs. Cover and refrigerate for 4 hours, turning the ribs over a few times.
> Grill ribs over medium-high heat until well done (about 6 minutes on each side), brushing with marinade often.

Bab — Korean Cooked Rice

Serves 4 to 6

1½ cups medium-grain white rice, soaked for 1 hour and drained

2½ cups water

Place rice and water in a saucepan and bring to boil. Reduce heat to low and cover. Cook for 15 minutes, stirring a number of times then re-covering. Stir, then re-cover and turn off heat. Let stand for 30 minutes.

Honeyed Rice with Nuts

Serves 4 to 6

2 tablespoons cooking oil
½ cup slivered almonds
½ cup pine nuts
4 cups hot cooked medium-grain white rice
4 tablespoons liquid honey
2 tablespoons soy sauce

Heat oil in a frying pan, then sauté almonds and pine nuts until they begin to brown. Stir in remaining ingredients, then serve warm.

Kong Jang
Black Bean Potage

Serves 4 to 6

1 cup dried black beans, soaked overnight and drained

5 cups water

2 tablespoons grated fresh ginger

5 tablespoons soy sauce

2 tablespoons firmly packed brown sugar

1 tablespoon toasted sesame seeds

Place beans, water, and ginger in a saucepan, then bring to boil. Cover and cook over medium-low heat for 2 hours or until the beans are well cooked, stirring a number of times and adding more water if necessary. Stir in remaining ingredients, except sesame seeds, then transfer into a serving bowl. Let cool. Garnish with sesame seeds and serve.

Dahk-Jlim
Chicken Stew

Serves 6 to 8

2 pounds boneless chicken breast, cut into serving pieces

4 medium potatoes, peeled and diced into ½-inch cubes

4 medium carrots, quartered lengthwise then cut into pieces 1 inch long

2 medium onions, finely chopped

1 small fresh hot pepper, seeded and finely chopped

6 garlic cloves, crushed

5 tablespoons soy sauce

2 tablespoons grated fresh ginger

1 teaspoon salt

1 teaspoon black pepper

5 cups water

Place all ingredients in a saucepan and bring to boil. Cover and cook over medium-low heat for 1 hour or until chicken is well done, stirring a number of times and adding more water if necessary. Place in a serving bowl, then serve hot.

Korean Chicken Soup

Serves 6 to 8

8 cups chicken broth

6 cloves garlic, crushed

2 tablespoons grated fresh ginger

½ cup medium-grain white rice, rinsed

4 tablespoons soy sauce

⅛ teaspoon cayenne pepper

2 cups shredded cooked chicken

½ cup finely chopped green onion

1 tablespoon sesame seeds, lightly toasted

❯ *Place chicken broth, garlic, ginger, and rice in a large saucepan, then bring to boil. Cover and cook over medium-low heat for 15 minutes. Add soy sauce, cayenne pepper, and chicken, then re-cover and cook for a further 5 minutes.*
❯ *Pour soup into bowls. Garnish with green onion and sesame seeds and serve.*

Sokkori Kuk
Oxtail Soup

Serves 6 to 8

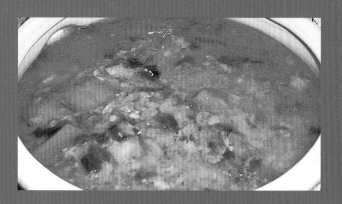

4 tablespoons cooking oil

2 pounds oxtail, cut into pieces

8 cups water

2 medium onions, finely chopped

1 cup finely chopped green onion

2 medium carrots, quartered lengthwise
then cut into 1-inch pieces

6 garlic cloves, crushed

2 teaspoons salt

A hearty soup with good flavor because of the long cooking process, I recommend it highly for cold winter days. Oxtail can be purchased at most butchers and meat departments in supermarkets.

Heat oil in a saucepan and brown oxtail pieces over medium heat for 10 minutes. Add water and bring to boil, then cover and simmer over medium-low heat for 2 hours or until oxtail is almost cooked. Add remaining ingredients, then cook for 1 hour or until meat and carrots are well cooked, adding more water if necessary.

Ho Baechu
Spiced Cabbage

Serves 4

4 cups shredded cabbage

1 tablespoon light sesame oil

2 garlic cloves, crushed

2 teaspoons sesame seeds

½ teaspoon black pepper

⅛ teaspoon cayenne pepper

2 tablespoons *Kimchi*

❯ *Place cabbage in a saucepan and cover with water. Bring to boil. Cook over medium heat for 3 minutes, then drain and set aside.*
❯ *Heat oil in a heavy frying pan or wok. Add cabbage and stir in remaining ingredients. Stir-fry for 1 minute, then serve immediately.*

Saewoo Jeon — Fried Shrimp

Serves about 4

¼ cup white flour

1½ teaspoons garlic powder

¾ teaspoon salt

½ teaspoon black pepper

Cooking oil

1 pound peeled and deveined raw shrimp

1 egg, beaten in a small bowl

> Combine flour, garlic powder, salt, and pepper in a small bowl and set aside.
> Pour oil to about 1 inch deep in a frying pan and heat over medium. Dredge shrimp in flour mixture, then dip in the egg. Deep-fry until golden brown. Drain on paper towels. Serve with soy sauce.

Ttok'wach'ae
Rice-Ball Fruit Cup

Serves about 6

½ cup rice flour

¼ teaspoon salt

2½ cups water

Raisins

Pine nuts

½ cup sugar

1 knob fresh ginger

1 medium apple, chopped into bite-size pieces

1 large plum, chopped into bite-size pieces

2 fresh apricots, chopped into bite-size pieces

> Knead the rice flour, salt, and ¼ cup of the water into a smooth dough, adding more water or flour if necessary, then shape into flat, chestnut-size pieces. Place two raisins and two pine nuts on each piece and re-shape into round balls.
> Place remainder of the water in a saucepan, then bring to boil. Add balls, then boil over medium-low heat for 10 minutes or until cooked. Remove balls with a slotted spoon and place in cold water for a few minutes, then drain.
> Place sugar and ginger in the still-boiling water and cook for 10 minutes over low heat to make a syrup. Allow to cool, then remove ginger from syrup. Place balls and fruit pieces in a bowl. Pour the syrup over the mixture and serve.

CHAPTER 9

The Food of Beijing

CHINA'S ROYAL FOOD

Beijing has developed one of the most important cuisines in the world. For centuries, this northern city was the royal capital of China, considered by its inhabitants to be the center of the world. With such a high regard for their country, it is no wonder that the Chinese developed a world-renowned cuisine epitomized by the Beijing kitchen.

For some 500 years, dynasty after dynasty came, conquered, and made Beijing their capital, each enriching it with new culinary attributes. The Liao, Jin, Yuan, Ming, and Qing or Manchu dynasties brought with them their culinary traditions when they came to power. Along with nomadic tribes who, at times, took over the city and added their bit to the creation of Beijing cookery, a cuisine was born that was to become known as the Royal Kitchen of China.

Within the walls of the larger city, the emperors built a royal city, known as the Forbidden City, from whence they ruled their empire. Some 20,000 of the best chefs in China worked in the kitchens of emperors. They had at their command the best food in the country and the means to acquire whatever they needed. With this power, they were able to create some of the most refined and delectable dishes in the world. From their famously grand and elaborate banquets, where it was not uncommon to find (besides the main dishes) 200 cold dishes and dozens of drinks and pastries, a rich culinary tradition was born.

Known as Shandong or Mandarin but more commonly as Beijing cuisine, this kitchen of the past, developed for royalty, today encompasses a major part of Chinese cuisine. The cooks for the Mongolian emperors and other rulers from the north created their basic food from meats, producing Beijing's most famous and renowned dishes. These were embellished with local foods, including those of the Muslims from the other regions of the country. They were brought to the capital by way of foreign merchants, vassal embassies, literati, and important court officials.

The Beijing kitchen continued to evolve after the era of emperors. Today, the city offers its traditional dishes as well as a wide range of international cuisine. Western visitors exploring the streets can find French, Italian, and Russian restaurants as well as Indian and Korean, and even the fast foods of North America such as Kentucky Fried Chicken, McDonalds, Pizza Hut, and others. These modern foreign introductions cannot compare with the food of the emperors, made to satisfy the royal families. Traditional Beijing dishes such as Beijing duck and hot-pot remain the main food items on the menu of the locals.

Mutton plays a major role in the Beijing kitchen. The Mongolian emperors and the privileged class of the Yuan Dynasty were enamored with mutton. In fact, it is estimated that 80 percent of their dishes were based on that meat, including instant-boiled mutton (mutton hot-pot), quick-fried mutton tripe, and stewed mutton—all still popular in Beijing and the surrounding region.

Rice is not very important in Beijing cuisine. Wheat products such as baked, fried, or steamed breads, as well as dumplings, noodles, and pancakes, are served more often than rice in Beijing restaurants. Wheat products are of prime importance in the culinary art of the city, and restaurant owners have used this fact to enhance their establishments. Visitors in noodle restaurants are usually totally enchanted to see a demonstrator transforming a handful of dough into uniform noodles.

Northern China is a region of extremes. The summers are hot and dry and the winters are bitterly cold, with chilling Arctic winds blowing in from Mongolia and Manchuria. Because of this harsh climate, Beijing dishes tend to be substantial. Liberal uses of hardy vegetables that grow well in colder climates are the main produce in Beijing's dishes. Cabbage and root vegetables like potatoes and turnips are used most, flavored with bean paste, cilantro, leeks, garlic, ginger, peppers, and soy sauce.

Braising, deep-frying, instant boiling, roasting, stewing, and stir-frying are all used in northern China. The techniques used in these methods of cooking plus the flavorings have evolved to produce many thousands of dishes with special flavors unmatched by most other cuisines. It is said that the Beijing kitchen imparts delicious uniqueness to the art of Chinese cooking. The restaurants of Beijing are a gourmet paradise, offering the city's traditional dishes embellished with those from other regions in China and numerous other countries in the world. The city's food even beats the Great Wall in drawing travelers. They come to experience the cuisine of the Imperial Kitchen, a world of culinary taste and refinement.

From this famous cuisine we have taken a few traditional imperial dishes and streamlined them. Yet, even in this simplified form, they still exude royal ancestry.

Zhajiang Noodles

Serves about 6

4 tablespoons light sesame oil

4 garlic cloves, crushed

½ pound ground pork

3 tablespoons soy sauce

2 tablespoons hoisin sauce

½ teaspoon chili flakes

½ teaspoon salt

½ pound firm tofu, diced into ½-inch cubes

⅓ cup water

1 cup finely chopped green onion

1 cup finely chopped peeled cucumber

1 pound any type wheat noodles, cooked according to package instruction, then placed on a platter but kept warm

› Heat oil in frying pan, then add garlic and stir-fry over medium-high heat for 30 seconds.
› Add pork and stir-fry for a further 5 minutes, then add soy sauce, hoisin sauce, chili, and salt. Stir-fry for 2 minutes. Stir in tofu and water, then turn heat to medium-low and cover. Simmer for 5 minutes. Stir in onion and cucumber, then stir-fry for 30 seconds. Spread over noodles and serve.

Chinese Pancakes

Makes about 18

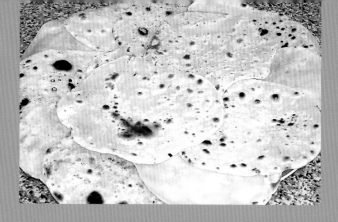

Beijing Duck (see page 73) is always served in this pancake.

2 cups white flour

¾ cup warm water

2 tablespoons light sesame oil

Knead flour and water into dough, then let stand for 1 hour. Form dough into 18 balls, then using a rolling pin, roll out into circles. Brush the top of the circles with sesame oil. Place one circle over the second one with the pancakes' oiled surfaces touching. Roll each pair of circles into a thin, 5-inch circle. Heat a greased pan, then fry over medium-low heat—1 minute on each side. Remove and separate into two while hot, then place on a platter. Cover to keep warm until use.

Hot and Sour Soup

Serves about 6

1 cup finely chopped cooked chicken

1 cup sliced small mushrooms

1 cup bean sprouts

4 tablespoons soy sauce

5 cups chicken broth

2 cups drained and chopped firm tofu

¾ teaspoon chili flakes

2 tablespoons white vinegar

2 tablespoons cornstarch, dissolved in 4 tablespoons water

1 egg, beaten

2 tablespoons light sesame oil

2 tablespoons finely chopped fresh cilantro

4 tablespoons finely chopped green onion

This soup is now famous worldwide—anywhere Chinese immigrants settled.

Place chicken, mushrooms, bean sprouts, soy sauce, and chicken broth in a saucepan, then bring to boil. Cover and cook over medium-low heat for 5 minutes. Stir in remaining ingredients except cilantro and green onion. Bring to boil, then cook over medium-low heat for about 3 minutes or until soup begins to thicken. Place in a serving bowl, then garnish with cilantro and green onion and serve.

• ASIAN COOKING MADE SIMPLE •

Mongolian Hot-Pot

Serves 4 to 6

1 pound boneless leg of lamb, cut into
paper-thin pieces 1 x 3 inches

Side dishes:

Soy sauce

Pickled garlic

Cilantro, finely chopped

Fermented bean curd

Chili flakes

Sesame paste

Pickled chive flowers

White vinegar

Hot water

4 tablespoons light sesame oil

1 piece fresh ginger (1 x ½ inch), thinly sliced

4 green onions, cut into 1-inch pieces

3 tablespoons soy sauce

In Beijing, hot-pot is a favorite of locals and foreigners alike. It's a cozy sight—people gathered around a small pot of boiling soup, dipping into it small pieces of meat and vegetables and cooking them in fondue-like fashion.

⟩ *Spread meat on individual plates.*
⟩ *Arrange the side dishes in small bowls.*
⟩ *Fill half of a 2 quart saucepan with hot water. Set on a hot plate on the diners' table, then add sesame oil, ginger, green onions, and 3 tablespoons of soy sauce. Bring to boil.*
⟩ *Serve by allowing diners to prepare their own private sauces in small bowls from the condiments in the side dishes. Diners then cook the lamb slices in the boiling water, dipping each slice less than 1 minute or until the meat turns pinkish-white. Diners dip the cooked slice into their personal sauce and enjoy.*

Beijing Dust

Serves 8

1 pound fresh chestnuts, scored

Water to cover

6 tablespoons sugar

1 teaspoon vanilla extract

2 cups whipping cream, whipped with 2 tablespoons fruit sugar

4 tablespoons chopped candied maraschino cherries

❯ Place chestnuts in a saucepan, then cover generously with water and bring to boil. Cook over medium heat for 50 minutes, then drain and allow to cool.

❯ Shell the chestnuts, then place chestnuts, sugar, and vanilla extract in a food processor and process for 30 seconds (do not puree). Divide the chestnuts into 8 dessert dishes, then spoon whipped cream over top. Decorate with cherries and serve.

Zha Jiang Mian
Beijing Noodles with Hot Meat Sauce

Serves about 6

1 pound udon noodles (or similar noodles such as spaghetti)

4 tablespoons light sesame oil

4 garlic cloves, crushed

1 pound ground beef

1 tablespoon grated fresh ginger

2 tablespoons soy sauce

2 tablespoons black bean sauce

1 tablespoon hot bean sauce

½ teaspoon salt

½ teaspoon black pepper

1 cup chicken broth

½ cup chopped green onion

1 teaspoon cornstarch, dissolved in 2 tablespoons water

Fresh cilantro, chopped

❯ Cook noodles according to directions on package, then place on a platter and keep warm.

❯ Heat oil in a frying pan, then add garlic, ground meat, and ginger. Stir-fry over medium heat until the meat browns—about 12 minutes. Stir in remaining ingredients, except cilantro, then bring to boil. Simmer over medium-low heat until sauce thickens, stirring a few times, then spread evenly over the noodles. Garnish with the cilantro and serve.

Beijing Duck

Serves about 6

1 whole duck (about 4 to 5 pounds), thoroughly cleaned

1 tablespoon cinnamon

1 tablespoon ground ginger

1½ teaspoons black pepper

1 teaspoon ground aniseed

½ cup liquid honey

2 tablespoons light sesame oil

2 tablespoons white vinegar

1 small bunch green onions, cut in half lengthwise then cut into 2- to 3-inch pieces

Hoisin sauce

Called the epitome of Chinese cuisine, Beijing Duck is traditionally served in three courses: a soup made from the bones of the duck as the first course; the second, duck pieces accompanied by pieces of crisp skin wrapped in Chinese Pancakes (see page 70) with sliced shallots and hoisin sauce (in restaurants usually only this course is served); and finally, a stir-fry of the remaining pieces of the duck. Usually made for a minimum of six people, Beijing Duck is prized, above all, for its crispy skin.

⟩ In a pot large enough to hold the duck, fill three-quarters full of water, then bring to boil. Remove from heat, then place duck in the boiling water for about 8 minutes. Remove duck and pat dry, then allow to stand for about 1 hour.

⟩ Place remaining ingredients, except green onions and hoisin sauce, in a saucepan. Bring to boil, then remove from heat and allow to cool.

⟩ Baste the duck all over, both inside and out, with the mixture, then allow to stand for 4 hours or until basting thoroughly dries on the duck.

⟩ Place duck, breast side up, in an oven preheated to 400° F. Roast for 30 minutes, then turn oven to 350° F and roast for another 30 minutes. Turn duck over again and roast for 15 minutes, then turn again and roast for a further 15 minutes. During these last 15 minutes, turn the duck over more often if need be to ensure that the skin browns evenly but does not burn. Serve duck pieces accompanied by pieces of crisp skin wrapped in Chinese pancakes with sliced green onions and hoisin sauce.

Beijing-Style Baked Eggs

Serves about 4

6 eggs, beaten

1 cup chopped cooked shrimp

½ cup fish stock

2 tablespoons light sesame oil

¾ teaspoon salt

½ teaspoon black pepper

1 tablespoon lemon juice

❯ *Preheat oven to 350° F.*
❯ *Thoroughly combine all ingredients, then place in a greased baking dish and bake uncovered for 30 minutes. Serve hot from baking dish.*

Beijing Five- Spice Chicken

Serves about 4

4 tablespoons Chinese stir-fry sauce

4 garlic cloves, crushed

½ teaspoon salt

¼ teaspoon cinnamon

¼ teaspoon ground cloves

¼ teaspoon ground fennel seeds

¼ teaspoon ground aniseed

¼ teaspoon chili flakes

3 tablespoons light sesame oil

2 pounds chicken wings or legs

This modern dish is very simple to prepare.

❯ *Combine sauce, garlic, salt, the five spices (cinnamon, cloves, fennel seed, aniseed, and chili flakes), and oil. Coat chicken wings or legs with the mixture and marinate for 4 hours.*
❯ *Preheat oven to 350° F.*
❯ *Place chicken wings or legs with their juice side by side in a greased baking dish. Cover and bake for 40 minutes. Uncover, then turn over and bake for a further 30 minutes. Serve with cooked rice and juice from the baking dish.*

Note: *The five spices included in this recipe can be found as a mixture in Asian food outlets and specialty food stores. Use 1¼ teaspoons of this mixture in this recipe.*

Mongolian Lamb

Serves 4 to 6

Marinade:

4 tablespoons soy sauce

4 tablespoons dry white wine

2 pounds lamb, thinly sliced then cut pieces 2 x 1 inch

Sauce:

4 tablespoons light sesame oil

1 teaspoon sugar

1 teaspoon black pepper

1 teaspoon ground ginger

1 tablespoon white vinegar

4 garlic cloves, sliced

1 cup chopped green onion

For the marinade:

❭ Combine 1 tablespoon of the soy sauce and 1 tablespoon of the wine.

❭ Thoroughly mix meat with the marinade and allow to marinate for 2 hours, turning the pieces over a few times.

For the sauce:

Combine the remaining soy sauce and wine, 2 tablespoons of the sesame oil, sugar, pepper, ginger, and vinegar, then set aside.

Heat remaining oil over high heat, then add garlic and stir-fry for about 30 seconds. Add meat and meat juices and stir-fry for a further 2 minutes. Add sauce and bring to boil, then stir in green onion. Stir-fry for another 3 minutes or until sauce is mostly absorbed. Serve hot.

CHAPTER 10

Cantonese Cuisine

THE MOST WELL-KNOWN OF CHINESE CUISINE

Cantonese is the most popular Chinese cuisine worldwide. Originating in Canton, in the Guangdong province in southern China, this tasty food is one of the main subdivisions of Chinese cuisine. The city of Canton, called Guangzhou in Chinese, has for centuries been one of the most important trading ports in China. This trade allowed a good number of Canton's citizens to be exposed to other nations of the world and gave them hope for opportunity elsewhere. For more than a century, Cantonese have been immigrating to other countries, especially to Canada and the United States. Because of this, Cantonese food was the first type of Chinese food to take hold in North America.

Chinese immigrants from the Canton region have been coming to Canada and the United States since the end of the nineteenth century. For years, they were subjected to discrimination such as paying a poll tax and facing prejudice in employment. Yet they had to find ways to make a living. In the prairie towns of western Canada, for example, they opened hand laundries, a job not many Canadians wanted to do. Later they opened restaurants, most serving Canadian dishes. However, in their kitchens at home they ate the tasty dishes of Canton. Having an inferiority complex in a world of colonialism, they did not think that their food was good enough for Canadians.

As the eating habits of Canadians began to evolve, the Chinese immigrants began to serve traditional Chinese dishes in their restaurants, and Cantonese cuisine began to make inroads into the Canadian kitchens. For those few restaurants in the larger towns of southern Saskatchewan that did serve Chinese food, although not knowing it then, what they served were Cantonese dishes. From that time onward, I was addicted to the delicious food of southern China. This love affair with Chinese food has grown, and today I prepare the foods of Canton and those of other parts of China.

Located on the Pearl River, Canton today is a major seaport set in the midst of endless rice paddies thriving in a tropical climate, turning Guangdong province into a major agricultural region. Hence, the ingredients for a rich cuisine are close at hand, making it, as some food writers indicate, the "haute cuisine of China."

All types of meats and fresh vegetables are used in Cantonese cuisine. Due to Canton's location edging the South China Sea, the city's specialty is fresh seafood dishes. The two favorite cooking methods are steaming and stir-frying. However, at times the dishes are double boiled, braised, or deep-fried.

Fats, herbs, and spices are used in moderation in Cantonese cooking. The ingredients for a dish are usually purchased the same day and cooked just before serving. Nothing is more tantalizing than the intoxicating aroma of fresh ingredients rising from steaming-hot Cantonese dishes.

Cantonese cuisine includes a good number of condiments and sauces. Ingredients such as garlic (used heavily in some dishes), chile peppers, five-spice powder, ginger, oyster sauce, rice wine, sesame oil, soy sauce, sugar, and star anise are used to enhance flavor.

Soup is usually a clear broth prepared by boiling meats and vegetables over a low fire for a long period of time. Only the liquid is consumed—the solids are usually thrown away. A somewhat different soup is the famous Cantonese shark fin soup, considered a highly prized delicacy but, today, very expensive to make. Since a good many species of sharks are now endangered, leading to the banning of shark finning in many parts of the world, the availability of shark fin soup has decreased immensely. Cantonese soups in their endless varieties are all, in my view, appetizing and go well with other foods. The Cantonese have a saying: "To keep a husband happy, a Cantonese wife needs to be able to cook good soups."

Above all, the Cantonese custom par excellence in the culinary world is the serving of dim sum ("to touch the heart"). In restaurants, these Cantonese snacks are usually served for breakfast or brunch. They commonly consist of tidbits such as gow (dumpling), steamed pork spare ribs, steamed buns with roast pork, and spring rolls, offered via cart service from steaming bamboo baskets to the customers' tables. One can order whatever pleases the eye. Dim sum is part of Cantonese life, and wherever immigrants from that part of China settle, it is common to see in Cantonese restaurants whole families enjoying their dim sums on Sunday mornings.

These few dishes do not do justice to tasty Cantonese cuisine, but they are simple to prepare, providing you with a taste of Cantonese food.

Cantonese Baked Chicken Wings

Serves 6 to 8

3 pounds chicken wings

4 tablespoons oyster sauce

2 tablespoons soy sauce

2 tablespoons black bean sauce

4 tablespoons dry red wine

1 tablespoon sugar

1 tablespoon light sesame oil

2 garlic cloves, crushed

1 medium onion, grated

½ teaspoon black pepper

½ teaspoon dry mustard

½ teaspoon oregano

This dish can be served cold or hot as an appetizer, as a snack, or even as an entrée.

› Preheat oven to 350°F.
› Spread the chicken wings in a greased baking dish, then set aside. In a bowl, thoroughly combine all the remaining ingredients. Brush the chicken wings on both sides with about a third of the mixture. Bake uncovered for 1½ hours or until the wings are well done, turning wings over at least once and brushing them with the mixture. Place in a serving platter, then brush with pan juices and serve.

Cantonese Pork and Shrimp

Serves 4

4 tablespoons light sesame oil

2 garlic cloves, crushed

¾ teaspoon salt

1 pound boneless pork or lamb, cut into very small pieces

1 pound tiger shrimp, peeled and deveined

2 tablespoons oyster sauce

2 tablespoons soy sauce

¾ cup hot water

2 teaspoons cornstarch, diluted in 4 tablespoons water

2 eggs, beaten

This dish is also delicious using lamb in place of pork.

Heat oil in a frying pan over high, then add garlic and salt. Stir-fry for 1 minute. Add meat, then stir-fry over medium heat until light brown. Stir in shrimp and stir-fry over medium-high heat for 3 minutes. Stir in oyster sauce, soy sauce, and hot water. Cover and cook over low heat for 5 minutes. Stir in cornstarch mixture and eggs; continue stirring for 1 minute. Serve with cooked rice.

Yao Gai — Soy Chicken

Serves 4 to 6

4 cinnamon sticks (about 2 inches each)

½ teaspoon ground aniseed

1 tablespoon grated fresh ginger

2 tablespoons firmly packed brown sugar

2 cups chicken broth

1 teaspoon garlic powder

3 tablespoons soy sauce

2 tablespoons dry white or red wine

2 pounds boneless chicken breasts, cut into ½-inch cubes

This very popular dish would traditionally be made with a whole chicken, usually served with stir-fried greens.

> *Place the cinnamon, aniseed, ginger, sugar, and chicken broth in a saucepan, then cover and bring to a boil over high heat. Add remaining ingredients and re-cover, then bring back to boil. Reduce heat to medium-low and simmer for 40 minutes, adding water if necessary. Turn off heat, but leave cover on and let stand on element for 1 hour.*
> *Remove and discard the cinnamon sticks. Serve with cooked rice and cooked greens.*

Cantonese Fried Rice

Serves about 8

3 tablespoons vegetable oil

1 medium onion, finely chopped

2 garlic cloves, crushed

4 eggs, beaten

1 cup cooked ham, cut into very small pieces

4 cups cooked medium- or long-grain white rice

1 cup sliced small mushrooms

1 cup sliced water chestnuts

4 tablespoons toasted slivered almonds

2 cups bean sprouts

4 tablespoons soy sauce

This tasty rice dish is often made with leftover meat and vegetables. All types of meats can be used, including ham, grilled pork, chicken, or lamb. It was the first dish that I enjoyed when I ventured into the Chinese culinary world.

Heat oil in a large heavy frying pan or wok, then stir-fry onion and garlic over medium-high heat for 3 minutes. Push onion and garlic to one side, then add eggs on the other side. Stir-fry eggs for 1 minute, then combine the onion, garlic, and eggs. Stir in the remaining ingredients except bean sprouts and soy sauce. Stir and toss until evenly mixed—about 2 minutes. Stir in bean sprouts and soy sauce, then stir-fry for 1 minute and serve.

Gai Lan
Broccoli with Oyster Sauce

Serves 4 to 6

1 pound Chinese or regular broccoli, cut into 1-inch pieces

1 teaspoon salt

1 teaspoon baking soda

1 teaspoon grated fresh ginger

4 tablespoons chicken broth

3 tablespoons oyster sauce

2 tablespoons red wine

1 teaspoon sugar

½ teaspoon garlic powder

This dish can be prepared with other Chinese greens such as bok choy.

❯ *Place broccoli, salt, baking soda, and ginger in a saucepan. Cover with water, then bring to boil and cover. Cook until the broccoli is tender, about 5 minutes. Drain, then rinse in cold water and drain again. Place in a serving platter and set aside.*
❯ *Combine all the remaining ingredients in a small saucepan and bring to boil. Remove from heat and pour evenly over the broccoli and serve immediately.*

Cantonese Almond Chicken

Serves about 6

Sauce:

1 tablespoon cornstarch, dissolved in 2 tablespoons water

2 tablespoons soy sauce

½ cup chicken broth

¼ cup white grape juice

2 teaspoons sugar

Chicken:

1 pound boneless chicken breast, cut into ½-inch cubes

4 tablespoons thinly sliced leeks

2 garlic cloves, crushed

1 teaspoon grated fresh ginger

3 tablespoons soy sauce

4 tablespoons peanut or olive oil

1 cup water chestnuts, drained and sliced

1 cup sliced mushrooms

2 cups (cut into ½-inch pieces) snow peas

½ cup lightly toasted almonds

I have dined on different versions of this dish for years, and I still look forward to eating it each and every time.

To prepare the sauce:
Make a sauce by combining all the sauce ingredients in a small bowl. Set aside.

To prepare the chicken:
> *Combine chicken, leeks, garlic, ginger, and soy sauce in a bowl. Let stand for 30 minutes.*
> *Heat oil in a wok or heavy frying pan, then stir-fry chicken with its marinade over medium-high heat for 4 minutes. Stir in water chestnuts, mushrooms, and snow peas, then stir-fry for 3 minutes. Stir in the sauce, then stir-fry for a further 3 minutes.*
> *Place on a serving platter. Spread almonds over top and serve hot with cooked rice or noodles.*

Spareribs with Black Bean Sauce

Serves 6

Marinade Sauce:

2 tablespoons soy sauce

3 tablespoons black bean sauce

2 tablespoons red wine

1 tablespoon sugar

⅛ teaspoon cayenne pepper

2 tablespoons light sesame oil

2 teaspoons ground ginger

3 garlic cloves, crushed

3 pounds pork spareribs

½ cup chicken broth

Probably what makes these ribs so tasty is the overnight marinating process, which makes them extremely flavorful and tender. Beef or chicken can be used as substitutes.

For the marinade sauce:
Combine all ingredients and set aside.

❯ *Place spareribs in a greased baking dish. Brush heavily on both sides with about a third of the sauce. Cover and refrigerate the remaining sauce and the ribs, allowing ribs to marinate overnight.*
❯ *Preheat oven to 350° F.*
❯ *Spoon the chicken broth over the ribs. Cover and bake for 2 hours or until ribs are well cooked, basting every 30 minutes with the remaining marinade sauce. For darker and crispier ribs, remove the cover for the last 30 minutes of baking.*
❯ *Cut ribs into sections. Serve warm with cooked rice and a little of the pan sauce.*

Chestnut Pudding

Serves 4 to 6

2 cups roasted and shelled chestnuts

2 cups warm water

⅔ cup sugar

½ cup cold water

½ cup milk

1 tablespoon cornstarch, dissolved in 2 tablespoons cold water

½ teaspoon almond extract

Whipped cream

Without the cornstarch and with less sugar, this pudding becomes a sweet soup, the way it is usually served in Canton. However, I have re-created it into a tasty pudding.

❯ *Puree chestnuts and warm water in a blender until smooth. Set aside.*
❯ *In a small saucepan, add the sugar and cold water and bring to boil. Turn the heat to low and slowly stir in chestnut puree. Continue to stir to ensure that chestnuts are not sticking to bottom of saucepan. Bring to boil, then stir in milk, dissolved cornstarch, and almond extract. Stirring constantly, cook until thickened.*
❯ *Place in 4 to 6 dessert cups and let cool. Top with whipped cream and serve.*

Beef with Oyster Sauce

Serves 4 to 6

1 pound beef round steak, cut into thin slices (about ½ x 2 inches)

2 tablespoons soy sauce

2 tablespoons dry red wine

1 tablespoon cornstarch, dissolved in 2 tablespoons water

¼ cup water

1 tablespoon firmly packed brown sugar

3 tablespoons oyster sauce

4 tablespoons peanut or olive oil

1 teaspoon grated fresh ginger

1 medium carrot, thinly sliced

1 cup sliced mushrooms

½ pound baby spinach, chopped into large pieces

½ teaspoon salt

½ teaspoon black pepper

⅛ teaspoon cayenne pepper

Oyster sauce enhances the natural flavor of meat.

❯ *Combine meat, soy sauce, wine, and cornstarch, then let stand for 30 minutes. Mix the water, sugar, and oyster sauce. Set aside. Preheat a wok over medium-high heat, then add 2 tablespoons of oil. Add ginger and stir-fry for 30 seconds, then stir in the meat with its marinade and stir-fry for 4 minutes or until almost cooked. Remove the beef slices from the wok.*

❯ *Add remaining oil to the wok, then stir-fry carrot for 2 minutes over medium-high heat. Stir in the mushrooms and spinach. Push vegetables to the sides, add the oyster sauce mixture in the middle, and bring to boil. Add beef slices, salt, pepper, and cayenne pepper, then stir-fry for 1 minute. Serve with cooked rice.*

Steamed Cantonese-Style Fish

Serves 4

2 to 3 pounds salmon or similar fish steaks

1½ teaspoons salt

2 tablespoons finely grated fresh ginger

4 tablespoons finely chopped green onion

1 small red sweet pepper, seeded and cut into thin strips

4 tablespoons light soy sauce

2 tablespoons peanut oil

3 teaspoons light sesame oil

2 tablespoons finely chopped fresh cilantro

This delicious dish is healthy and low in fat. It has been one of my favorites from the time I first ate it in a small Chinese restaurant in Regina, Saskatchewan.

❯ *Rub fish steaks with salt. Place fish in the perforated upper pan of a double boiler, then set aside.*
❯ *Fill the lower pan of the double boiler with water and bring to boil. Nestle the upper pan (with the fish) over the lower pan. Spread ginger over the fish.*
❯ *Allow fish to steam over high heat for 10 to 15 minutes. It is cooked when the fish begins to flake slightly but still remains moist.*
❯ *Remove the steamed fish and place on a platter. Spread the green onion and red pepper slices over top, then drizzle with the soy sauce.*
❯ *Heat the peanut and sesame oils in a small saucepan until they begin to smoke, then immediately pour them over the fish. Spread cilantro over top and immediately serve with cooked rice.*

CHAPTER 11

The Dishes of Xi'an

NORTHERN CHINA'S GOURMET FOOD

On the second day that we were in Xi'an, the city that gave birth to China, we decided to try the epitome of the city's renowned cuisine. Seated in the Shaanxi Grand Opera Theatre, we anxiously waited for our meal to begin. Soon our waiter was bringing bamboo trays filled with dish after dish of steamed jiaozis (dumplings) in all shapes and forms. It was a gourmet parade, a fine introduction to Xi'an cuisine. Situated strategically at the crossroads of the routes across China and Central Asia, the city of Xi'an grew into one of the most sophisticated and wealthy urban centers in the world during the Classical Period and the Middle Ages. In those centuries, it was also the first Chinese city to open its doors to the outside world. It established itself as a world leader in culture and trade and became the first stop on the famous Silk Road, playing a vital role in bridging the gap between East and West. From here, caravans began their journeys westward and returned with products and new ideas from India, Persia, the Arab world, and beyond. It also became the home of traders from all over the civilized world, who brought with them the Buddhist, Christian, and Muslim religions and the food of their homelands. Through the years, much of the culinary delights of Asia and the Middle East were incorporated into Xi'an cooking, creating a unique and tasty cuisine. Xi'an reached the peak of its culture and power during the Tang Dynasty (A.D. 618–907) when the city became one of the most important centers of the then known world. The Silk Road activities and the renowned cuisine, along with the famous Terracotta Army, created to protect the spirit of one of China's most renowned emperors, Qin Shi Huang, have made the city a tourist destination par excellence. The caravan trade gave birth to the Muslim Quarter in the heart of the city. Adding an element of architectural diversity to the town's structures, it has become the core of Xi'an's outstanding foods. The 30,000 mostly Muslim inhabitants of the Quarter, said to be descendants of eighth-century Arab soldiers, make the city an exotic combination of China and the Middle East. At the heart of this ancient section of the city, surrounded by well-preserved medieval walls, is the Daqinzhan Si (Great Mosque), the largest and oldest of the ten mosques in the city. First built in A.D. 742, it is a superb example of Sino-Arab architecture. Its minaret, in the shape of an octagonal pagoda, overlooks the old houses of the Quarter. The only mosque open to foreigners, it edges narrow Middle Eastern-style streets and is surrounded by a combination of Arab and old Chinese buildings.

Around the mosque and beyond, wonderful local Muslim food is offered in hundreds of eating places, from street food stalls to fine restaurants. There are few other spots in the city that can match this area, which stretches a few hundred meters or yards from the Drum Tower. Called the "Food Street of the City," it has countless eateries, including pastry and nut shops. At night, temporary food stands line both sides of the street, infusing the air with the delicious aroma of barbecuing kaoyangrou (lamb or mutton on skewers) and steaming dumpling dishes. It is an exciting event that offers travelers the chance to sample the culinary delights offered by these stalls in this romantic and historic part of Xi'an.

The city also has a long history of specializing in the dishes of northwestern China, foods that have been influenced by the Hui people (Chinese Muslims). At the top of these are the city's specialties, yangrou paomo (steamed bun in mutton soup) and innumerable types of jiaozis. Wheat noodles and steamed bread are more popular than rice, and lamb and mutton are the preferred meats. Most eateries serve hefty portions, and prices are very reasonable.

There are numerous restaurants in the Muslim Quarter that cater toward visitors. Among these is the high-class Xi'an Restaurant, noted for its recipes in the style of the royal court. The waitstaff usually tells diners a story or an anecdote related to each dish served. The other two restaurants frequented by tourists are the Tong Sheng Xiang, noted for its mutton soup, and De Fa Chang—known for its shark fin jiaozis—where the food is even better and more reasonably priced. As we relished our seemingly never-ending jiaozis,

I could not believe the variety served: sixteen types are usually offered as appetizers with a meal but, at times, 800 are served at a feast. All were delicious, delicate, and inviting in appearance. They came in countless shapes, such as avocados, chicken, cauliflowers, crabs, ducks, and endless other versions, with each form reflecting the filling. My favorites were those shaped like walnuts. To me they were tastier than the real nut. The jiaozis were still coming when a show began. The food had been heavenly, but what followed was a real competition. The stunning costumes, music, songs, and dances of the performers reflected those of the Tang Dynasty and are said to be the best in China. They seemed to be the most delightful in the world. I was overwhelmed by their beauty, delicacy, and splendor of performance. I can honestly say that the show was the icing that topped our superb dinner.

To convey some of the excellence of Xi'an foods that I enjoyed, I have changed to my own taste and simplified, to some extent, a number of the following dishes that I thoroughly enjoyed during my sojourn in Xi'an.

Fish and Scallops

Serves 6 to 8

2 tablespoons soy sauce

1 tablespoon Ginger Sauce (see page 87)

½ cup finely chopped onion

1 pound any solid-type fish fillet, cut into 2-inch squares

4 tablespoons vegetable oil

½ pound fresh scallops, dipped in boiling water for 2 minutes, then drained

> Combine soy sauce, Ginger Sauce, and onions, then coat fish squares with mixture and place in a bowl. Let stand for 20 minutes, turning fish over once or twice.
> Heat oil in a frying pan, then sauté fish over medium-high heat for 4 minutes, turning them over once. Add the scallops, then gently stir-fry for 2 minutes and serve.

You Tiau — Chinese Crullers

Makes 18

1 pound of bread dough

Oil for deep-frying

Much simplified from the original version, these crullers can be eaten as appetizers or as bread with soups and stews.

> Form dough into about 18 balls, then roll each into a cylinder shape ½-inch in diameter. Cover with a cloth towel, then let stand for 1 hour. Pour oil in a saucepan to about ½ inch deep, then heat over medium. Holding a dough cylinder with fingers at both ends, twist and pull to create an elongated twist. Drop into the oil, then deep-fry until golden brown. Repeat for each cylinder.
> Remove twists with a slotted spoon and place on paper towels. Serve warm.

Nectarine Salad with Ginger Vinaigrette Dressing

Serves 6 to 8

4 tablespoons peanut oil

¼ cup thin strips of fresh ginger

2 tablespoons grated fresh ginger

4 tablespoons white vinegar

1 tablespoon sugar

½ teaspoon salt

½ teaspoon black pepper

2 medium nectarines, cut into thin slices

12 water chestnuts, peeled and thinly sliced

6 cups chopped lettuce

> Heat oil in a frying pan until it sizzles, then stir in ginger strips. Fry for a few seconds until golden. Quickly strain and reserve oil, then place fried ginger strips aside and allow oil to cool.
> In a blender, process together the reserved oil, grated ginger, vinegar, sugar, salt, and pepper for 1 minute to make dressing.
> Toss nectarines, chestnuts, and lettuce in a serving bowl. Gently stir in dressing, then top with fried ginger and serve.

Ginger Sauce

Makes about 1 to 1½ cups

3 tablespoons grated fresh ginger

8 garlic cloves, crushed

2 tablespoons light sesame oil

3 tablespoons soy sauce

3 tablespoons white vinegar

1 teaspoon black pepper

1 teaspoon sugar

⅛ teaspoon cayenne pepper

2 tablespoons water

½ cup very finely chopped green onions

Served with mutton soup
and all types of *jiaozis*.

Combine all ingredients, then serve.

Soybean Milk Soup

Serves 4 to 6

2 tablespoons chopped dried shrimp

2 tablespoons soy sauce

2 teaspoons light sesame oil

2 teaspoons white vinegar

½ teaspoon black pepper

½ teaspoon salt

⅛ teaspoon cayenne pepper

4 cups soybean milk

4 tablespoons finely chopped green onion

4 tablespoons finely chopped fresh cilantro

Chinese Crullers (see page 86) or bread cubes

For those who cannot have dairy products, this
delicious soup is heaven-sent.

❯ *Place shrimp in a bowl and cover with water.
Allow to soak for 4 hours. Drain.*
❯ *Place all ingredients, except soybean milk,
green onion, cilantro, and Chinese Crullers
or bread cubes, in a serving bowl.*
❯ *Place soybean milk in a saucepan and boil over
medium heat. As soon as it boils, pour soybean
milk into the serving bowl. Thoroughly stir in
onion and cilantro.*
❯ *Serve with bread cubes or Chinese Crullers.*

Jiaozi – Dumplings

Makes 40 dumplings

Dough:

2 cups white flour

⅔ cup warm water

¼ teaspoon salt

Filling:

1 cup finely chopped cabbage

1 cup ground meat, any kind

½ cup finely chopped green onion

½ cup finely chopped mushrooms

2 tablespoons soy sauce

1 tablespoon grated fresh ginger

2 teaspoons sugar

2 tablespoons light sesame oil

2 teaspoons cornstarch

½ teaspoon salt

½ teaspoon black pepper

The preparation of *jiaozis* is a labor-intensive effort. For festive occasions, the whole family takes part in preparing the dumplings before they sit down to enjoy their creations. The dumplings can be stuffed with all types of meats and vegetables. They are usually served boiled in soups, pan-fried, or steamed on bamboo trays.

For the dough:

❯ *Knead together flour, warm water, and salt, adding more water or flour if necessary. Cover and allow to stand for 1 hour.*

For the filling:

❯ *Combine filling ingredients, then set aside.*
❯ *Form dough into about 40 balls, then roll out balls into rounds as thin as possible. Cover with a tea cloth. Place 1 heaping teaspoon of filling on the center of each round, then fold dough and pinch shut in a half moon shape or any other shape desired. Cook* jiaozis *one of three ways: deep-fry; steam on bamboo trays; or bring water in a saucepan to boil, add* jiaozis, *and cook for 10 minutes over medium-high heat before removing* jiaozis *with a slotted spoon.*
❯ *Serve immediately with Ginger Sauce (see page 87).*

Spicy Roast Chicken

Serves 4 to 6

1 chicken (about 4 pounds), thoroughly washed
4 tablespoons soy sauce
4 garlic cloves, crushed
2 tablespoons liquid honey
2 tablespoons white vinegar
½ teaspoon salt
1 teaspoon finely chopped fresh ginger
¼ teaspoon ground aniseed
¼ teaspoon cinnamon
¼ teaspoon ground fennel seeds
¼ teaspoon black pepper
¼ teaspoon ground nutmeg
¼ teaspoon ground cloves
¼ cup boiling water

❯ *Preheat oven to 400° F.*
❯ *Place chicken in roasting pan, then set aside.*
❯ *Combine remaining ingredients, then rub chicken (inside and out) with the mixture. Cover and roast for 30 minutes. Reduce heat to 350° F, then roast for 45 minutes or until the chicken is well cooked, basting several times with remaining basting juice and pan juices. Roast uncovered for 15 minutes, then serve.*

Heiheluo
Black Noodles

Serves about 4

¾ pound black noodles (spaghetti-like, or any type of wheat noodles)
2 tablespoons vegetable oil
1 large onion, finely chopped
1 large sweet pepper, seeded and finely chopped
1 small fresh hot pepper, seeded and finely chopped
½ teaspoon black pepper
3 tablespoons soy sauce

For the poor in Xi'an, this and similar noodle dishes are quite common fare. They can be cooked and served cold with all types of sauces or stir-fried with vegetables, as in this recipe.

❯ *Cook noodles according to instructions on package, then set aside.*
❯ *Heat oil in a heavy frying pan or wok, then stir-fry vegetables over medium-high heat until they turn limp. Stir in noodles, pepper, and soy sauce, then stir-fry for a few moments and serve.*

Yangrou Paomo — Bread and Mutton Soup

Serves 8

4 to 6 pounds mutton, lamb, or beef bones, broken into 4- to 5-inch pieces

2 medium onions, finely chopped

6 garlic cloves, crushed

1 small fresh hot pepper, seeded and finely chopped

1 tablespoon grated fresh ginger

Water

½ pound wheat noodles

2½ teaspoons salt

1 teaspoon black pepper

1 teaspoon ground cumin

½ pound lean lamb, very thinly sliced

1 cup finely chopped green onion

1 cup finely chopped cilantro

4 cups cubed day-old bread or Chinese Crullers (see page 86)

An Arab-influenced dish brought along the Silk Road, *paomo* is said to be the dish that made Xi'an a jewel in the Chinese culinary world. The unleavened bread in this dish is *mo*, a bread that, according to locals, was brought to the East by Arab traders thousands of years ago. The same is said about *Yangrou Paomo*.

❯ *Place bones, onions, garlic, hot pepper, and ginger in a large saucepan, then cover with water to 2 inches above bones. Bring to boil. Cover and cook over medium-low heat for 4 hours, adding more water if necessary.*
❯ *In the meantime, cook noodles according to directions on package and set aside.*
❯ *Strain and discard bones and vegetables, then return broth to saucepan, adding water if necessary (will need 8 cups total). Stir in salt, pepper, and cumin, then bring to boil and cook over medium heat for 5 minutes. Keep hot.*
❯ *Divide remaining ingredients, except bread, into 8 large soup bowls. Pour broth over ingredients and stir bread into each bowl. Serve hot.*

Barbecued Lamb Kebabs

Serves 6 to 8

3 pounds lamb, cut into 1-inch cubes

4 tablespoons soy sauce

4 tablespoons vegetable oil

2 tablespoons lemon juice

4 garlic cloves, crushed

1 teaspoon black pepper

1 teaspoon sugar

½ teaspoon ground fennel seeds

½ teaspoon ground nutmeg

⅛ teaspoon cayenne pepper

❯ *Thoroughly combine all ingredients in a bowl, then cover and refrigerate for about 2 hours.*

❯ *Place lamb cubes on skewers, then barbecue until meat lightly browns, basting with the juice of the marinade as the cubes are barbecuing. Serve hot.*

CHAPTER 12

Szechuan Cuisine:

THE GATEWAY TO CHINA

Szechuan cuisine is one of the most famous of China's regional culinary arts. Emphasizing the use of chile peppers, it is renowned for its sharp and spicy flavors. Szechuan cooks enhance their dishes further by the use of chile pepper oil, Szechuan peppercorn, sesame seeds, garlic, and ginger, as well as fermented soybeans and vegetables, adding myriad tastes to their dishes. It is said that one who has not enjoyed Szechuan food has never been to China. Located along the Yangtze and isolated by mountains, Szechuan has developed a strong regional identity. A land of beautiful lakes, hot springs, deep ravines, limestone caves, and waterfalls, it is known in China as the land of plenty. Szechuan is very fertile and produces abundant agricultural crops and a profusion of strong herbs and herb-like spices. Its cuisine is also the spiciest in China. This has given the inhabitants the reputation for being a bit spicy—local women are known as la mei zi, "spice girls."

The Szechuan kitchen, one of the world's great culinary traditions and one of the most emphatically flavored cuisines in all of China, was for centuries hidden to the outside world. However, in China it has always been legendary for its sophistication, richness, and diversity, boasting at least 5,000 different dishes. Today its fame is beginning to spread worldwide, and has become a very popular food among many non-Chinese.

Strangely, the chile pepper has had a great hand in the formation of Szechuan cuisine making this hot pepper so much in demand. Its use is so popular in this part of China, the standard belief being that Szechuan's humid climate encourages people to eat strongly spiced foods, as an aid in reducing internal dampness by allowing the body to sweat more.

Chili peppers are not native to Szechuan. They were introduced to China in the seventeenth century from the Americas. How these peppers reached landlocked Szechuan is not clear, but it is believed they were introduced from India when Chinese merchants met Portuguese and Spanish traders along the renowned Silk Road.

This does not mean that the Szechuan cook had no way of producing "the hot" before the discovery of the Americas. Even before the introduction of the chile, the people of Szechuan had developed what is called the Szechuan peppercorn, also known as pepper flower, Chinese pepper, and fagara.

Not a pepper at all, it is a reddish-brown fruit produced by the prickly ash tree and locally known as huajiao. It gives zest to any dish without overpowering the natural taste of the food. This fruit numbs the mouth, which imbues a unique taste.

It is no wonder this fine cuisine has become so important in the world of hot culinary dishes. Color, flavor, nutrition, shape, and smell are carefully balanced to make the nutritious dishes appealing.

Yet, even though hot mouth-burning food is what comes to mind when Szechuan dishes are mentioned, at least one-third of the Szechuan cuisine is barely spiced or not spiced at all. The balancing of taste, no doubt, also contributes to the fame of this important part of Chinese cuisine.

Szechuan cooks make use of numerous cooking methods, from braising, stir-frying, and boiling, to roasting, simmering, steaming, and stewing. A complete list would include more than twenty distinct techniques. Among the most important spicy dishes in the region are Szechuan-style hot pot, kung pao chicken fried with peanuts, spicy crab, smoked duck, mapo tofu, Szechuan pepper beef, and twice-cooked pork (pork is first boiled, then stir-fried). Beef is, to some degree, more common in Szechuan cooking than in other Chinese cuisines. Stir-fried beef is often cooked until chewy, while steamed beef is, at times, coated with rice flour to produce a rich gravy.

If novices wish to experiment in preparing the hot dishes of Szechuan, they will come to appreciate the notable characteristics of Szechuan cooking and its dazzling variety of flavors.

The following traditional Szechuan dishes, created to my own taste, have been simplified. Some of the spices, hard to find in North American markets, have been replaced with somewhat similar and more accessible spices.

Spicy Pepper Beef with Noodles

Serves 6 to 8

2 pounds round steak, sliced into thin strips

4 tablespoons soy sauce

4 tablespoons hoisin sauce

4 tablespoons water

1 tablespoon lemon juice

2 teaspoons sugar

1 teaspoon chili flakes

1 pound thin rice noodles

2 tablespoons light sesame oil

1 small bunch green onions, finely chopped

2 tablespoons sesame seeds

❯ Mix steak, soy sauce, hoisin sauce, water, lemon juice, sugar, and chili flakes in a bowl. Cover and refrigerate for 3 hours, stirring a number of times. Drain steaks, but reserve marinade. Set aside.

❯ Cook noodles according to instructions on package then drain. Stir 1 tablespoon of the sesame oil into the noodles, then set aside.

❯ Heat the remaining sesame oil in wok or large, heavy frying pan. Stir-fry steak until tender. Remove and set aside.

❯ Add onions and reserved marinade to wok or frying pan and stir until hot. Add steak, noodles, and sesame seeds and stir-fry for 2 minutes. Serve hot.

Szechuan Chicken

Serves 4 to 6

2 pounds boneless chicken breast, cut into bite-size pieces
½ cup cornstarch
4 tablespoons cooking oil
4 garlic cloves, crushed
5 tablespoons soy sauce
2 tablespoons white vinegar
¼ cup water
4 green onions, cut into pieces 1 inch long
½ teaspoon chili flakes

❯ Roll chicken pieces in the cornstarch.
❯ Heat oil in a wok, then stir-fry chicken and garlic until chicken lightly browns. Add soy sauce, vinegar, and water. Cover and cook over medium-low heat for 5 minutes or until chicken is done. Add green onions and chili flakes, then stir-fry for 2 minutes. Serve hot.

Szechuan Tuna or Salmon

Serves 6 to 8

2 pounds tuna or salmon fillet

Marinade:
1 teaspoon chili flakes
4 tablespoons soy sauce
4 tablespoons liquid honey
2 tablespoons water
1 tablespoon grated fresh ginger

Sauce:
3 tablespoons mayonnaise
2 tablespoons liquid honey
⅛ teaspoon cayenne pepper

Place tuna or salmon fillet in a baking dish.

For the marinade:
Combine the marinade ingredients and pour over steaks. Allow to marinate for 1 hour, turning the steaks over once or twice.

For the sauce:
Make a sauce by combining the sauce ingredients, then set aside.

Wrap fillet with aluminum foil. Barbecue over medium heat for about 10 minutes, turning fillet over once. Serve with sauce.

Szechuan Green String Beans

Serves about 6

Cooking oil
2 pounds green string beans, trimmed, broken in 1- to 2-inch pieces
½ pound ground pork
6 garlic cloves, crushed
4 tablespoons soy sauce
1 tablespoon sugar
½ teaspoon chili flakes
¼ cup water
2 teaspoons light sesame oil
1 cup chopped green onion

> In a saucepan, heat oil for deep-frying over medium-high. Deep-fry beans for 1 minute. Drain on paper towels.

> Heat 4 tablespoons oil in a heavy frying pan or wok, then stir-fry pork over medium-high heat for 4 minutes. Add beans and garlic. Stir-fry for a further 4 minutes. Stir in remaining ingredients and stir-fry for a further 2 minutes. Serve hot.

Bean Curd and Shrimp Soup

Serves about 8

6 cups chicken stock
¼ pound peeled and deveined shrimp
1 cup green peas
½ pound bean curd, cut into ½-inch cubes
4 tablespoons ¼-inch cubes of ham
2 tablespoons soy sauce
1 tablespoon finely chopped pickle
1 tablespoon cornstarch, dissolved in 1 cup water
1 egg, beaten
1 teaspoon salt
½ teaspoon black pepper

Boil chicken stock in a saucepan. Add shrimp, peas, bean curd, ham, soy sauce, and pickle. Bring to boil, then cover and cook over medium heat for 5 minutes. Add dissolved cornstarch, egg, salt, and pepper, then stir constantly until the soup begins to thicken. Serve immediately.

Szechuan Spicy Tofu

Serves 4 to 6

3 tablespoons light sesame oil

1 tablespoon grated fresh ginger

2 garlic cloves, crushed

4 tablespoons finely chopped green onion

2 tablespoons Szechuan hot bean paste

2 pounds extra firm tofu, cut into 1-inch cubes

2 tablespoons soy sauce

1 teaspoon sugar

½ teaspoon salt

½ cup water

1 tablespoon cornstarch, dissolved in 3 tablespoons water

⅛ teaspoon cayenne pepper

The Szechuan hot bean paste used in this recipe is available at most Asian groceries.

Heat oil in wok or frying pan, then stir-fry ginger, garlic, and 2 tablespoons of the green onion for 30 seconds over high heat. Add bean paste and tofu, then stir-fry for another 1 minute. Add soy sauce, sugar, salt, and water, and bring to boil. Stir in dissolved cornstarch and cayenne pepper. Stir-fry for 1 minute, then transfer to a serving platter. Decorate with remaining green onion and serve.

Szechuan Stir-Fried Shrimp

Serves 4

2 tablespoons tomato paste, dissolved in 4 tablespoons water

2 teaspoons white vinegar

2 teaspoons sugar

1 tablespoon soy sauce

¼ teaspoon salt

⅛ teaspoon cayenne pepper

2 tablespoons light sesame oil

4 garlic cloves, crushed

1 small onion, thinly sliced

2 cups sliced mushrooms

1 pound peeled and deveined shrimp

❯ *Thoroughly combine diluted tomato paste, vinegar, sugar, soy sauce, salt, and cayenne pepper to make a sauce, then set aside.*
❯ *Heat sesame oil in a wok or frying pan over medium-high, then add garlic, onion, and mushrooms. Stir-fry until onion becomes tender. Add shrimp and stir-fry until shrimp turn pink. Add sauce, then stir-fry for 2 minutes and serve.*

Szechuan Eggplant

Serves 4 to 6

2 tablespoons red bean paste

1 tablespoon soy sauce

2 teaspoons white vinegar

2 teaspoons sugar

½ teaspoon chili flakes

6 tablespoons light sesame oil

1 pound eggplant, peeled and cut into 2-inch wedges

2 garlic cloves, crushed

1 tablespoon grated fresh ginger

1 teaspoon cornstarch, dissolved in 1 tablespoon water

2 tablespoons finely chopped onion

❯ *Combine bean paste, soy sauce, vinegar, sugar, and chili flakes, then set aside.*
❯ *Heat sesame oil in a wok or frying pan, then add eggplant, garlic, and ginger. Stir-fry over medium-high heat for 5 minutes. Add red bean paste mixture, cornstarch, and onion, then stir-fry for 2 minutes and serve.*

General Tso's Chicken

Serves about 4

1 pound boneless chicken breast, cut into thin slices 2 inches long

3 tablespoons soy sauce

1 tablespoon grated fresh ginger

1 teaspoon cornstarch, dissolved in 1 tablespoon sesame oil

5 tablespoons light sesame oil

2 dried medium chile peppers, seeded and cut in half

2 tablespoons finely chopped orange rind

1 teaspoon sugar

Mix chicken, 2 tablespoons of the soy sauce, ginger, and dissolved cornstarch in a bowl. Allow to marinate for about 1 hour. Remove chicken and set aside. Heat sesame oil in wok or heavy frying pan over medium-high and stir-fry chicken for 4 minutes or until it begins to brown. Remove chicken with slotted spoon and drain on paper towels. Pour out the oil, reserving about 2 teaspoons. Re-heat the 2 teaspoons of oil, then stir-fry the chile for a few seconds. Add chicken, the remaining soy sauce, orange rind, and sugar, then stir-fry for 3 minutes. Serve immediately.

Szechuan Noodle Salad

Serves about 8

¼ pound thin rice noodles, cooked as indicated on package, drained, and cooled

2 cups cooked and shredded chicken

1 cup finely shredded cabbage

1 cup grated carrots

1 medium sweet pepper, seeded and finely chopped

½ cup finely chopped green onion

4 tablespoons light sesame oil

2 tablespoons soy sauce

2 tablespoons liquid honey

1 tablespoon white vinegar

2 tablespoons grated fresh ginger

1 teaspoon chili flakes

4 tablespoons toasted peanuts

❭ *Place noodles, chicken, cabbage, carrots, sweet pepper, and green onion in a large salad bowl and set aside.*
❭ *Combine remaining ingredients, except peanuts, to make a salad dressing. Stir into ingredients in salad bowl, then sprinkle with peanuts and serve.*

Note: *This makes an excellent vegetarian dish if the chicken is omitted.*

ASIAN COOKING MADE SIMPLE

CHAPTER 13

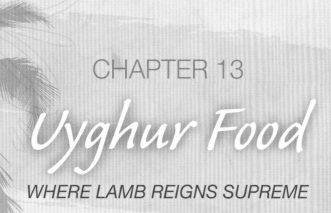

Uyghur Food

WHERE LAMB REIGNS SUPREME

During my travels in China I met an American tourist who had just visited Ürümqi, the capital of China's remote northwestern province of Xinjiang. When I asked him how he liked the food of the Uyghurs who inhabit that little-known part of the country, he replied, "It seemed to me that almost all the dishes that I ate were cooked with either mutton or lamb." The Uyghurs should call themselves "the people of the lamb."

This tourist coming from the western border of China had a point. Uyghur cooking mainly relies on lamb and mutton, a culinary art that has influenced other cuisines in the vast region of Central Asia. The ancient Silk Road that ran from China's Xinjiang province to Central Asia had a great hand in giving birth to the development of the Uyghur kitchen. In the ensuing centuries, Uyghur cuisine became famous, and it spread to the large urban centers in China, Central Asia, and beyond, as far away as Australia.

The majority of Uyghurs—sometimes spelled Uighur, Uigyur, or Uygur—live in Xinjiang, the Uyghur Autonomous Region of China. Large communities of Uyghurs, a Turkic people, are also located in the Central Asian countries of Afghanistan, Kazakhstan, Kyrgyzstan, Mongolia, Tadjikistan, Uzbekistan, and as far away as Turkey. China has fifty-six ethnic groups, and the Uyghurs are the country's largest minority.

The legendary commercial Silk Road, which ran through Xinjiang, had an overwhelming influence in the creation of Uyghur dishes. The trade route that ran from China to the Middle East and beyond carried the foods of the Far East to the Western world and the dishes of the Middle East to China. The Uyghurs, in the midst of this commerce, integrated the cuisine of East Asia with that of the Middle East, especially after the dawn of Islam and their conversion to that faith. Today, when dining on Uyghur dishes, a traveler is reminded of the foods of Damascus or Baghdad with more than a touch of the Chinese kitchen.

Uyghur cuisine is famous all over China for its lamb and mutton dishes. To the Uyghurs, lamb and mutton are the mother of all food, especially when it comes to their kebab dishes. These kebabs are popular throughout China and are a key food item sold in fast-food venues and other eateries all over Xinjiang. The aroma from the skewers of kebabs grilling over charcoal gives hunger pangs to any meat lover who inhales these enticing aromas.

The Uyghurs are also known for their noodles made by hand from flour, water, and salt with no use of machines. The dough is made into small balls, then stretched by hand. These types of noodles are the basis of such dishes as the famous traditional dish laghman. Foods used to a lesser extent in Uyghur cooking include meats such as beef, camel, chicken, and goose; vegetables like carrots, eggplant, tomatoes, onions, peppers, and celery; and dairy foods, noodles, rice, and fruits. There are also some forty types of bread, of which one always accompanies the meal. A number of them are eaten as snacks. Above all other foods, however, lamb reigns supreme in the Uyghur kitchen, and the dishes made from this meat are endless.

Seafood is not often found in Uyghur food due to the distance to the sea. The Guinness Book of Records states that Ürümqi is 2,500 kilometers (1,500 miles) from the sea, making it the world's farthest city from the ocean.

Some of the Uyghur dishes are quite hot and spicy because of the extensive use of chili flakes or cayenne pepper and other hot spices. Cumin is also a favorite. Other spices commonly used are coriander seed, ginger, pepper, and nutmeg.

The two most popular drinks are black tea and kvass, a non-alcoholic drink made with honey. Tea is taken for breakfast and is important in the social life of the Uyghurs, who like to serve guests this beverage along with nang (Uyghur bread, also called naan) and fruit before the main course of the meal.

It seems that besides being nourishing, Uyghur food is also healthy. The people of the Uyghur region in China have the highest longevity in the country. No doubt the environment and weather play a hand, but there is a sincere conviction that Uyghur cuisine has much to do with this long life. In their folklore, the people believe that the fat consumed with mutton and lamb is responsible for their long lives.

In this minuscule foray into the food of the Uyghurs, I have simplified the traditional recipes and substituted ingredients not easily found in Western food markets.

Shogoruq
Uyghur Nomad Soup

Serves about 10

4 tablespoons cooking oil
1 pound lamb meat, cut into ½-inch cubes
3 medium potatoes, peeled and diced into ½-inch cubes
1 medium carrot, diced into ½-inch cubes
1 large bell pepper, seeded and diced into ½-inch squares
1 medium onion, finely chopped
2 cups stewed tomatoes
1½ teaspoons salt
1 teaspoon ground cumin
1 teaspoon black pepper
1 teaspoon ground ginger
2 chicken bouillon cubes, dissolved in 8 cups water
3 teaspoons lemon juice
6 garlic cloves, finely chopped
4 tablespoons finely chopped fresh cilantro

A hearty soup such as *Shogorug* is what the Uyghur recommend for people who have a cold or the flu.

❯ *Heat oil in a saucepan, then sauté meat over medium heat for 8 minutes. Add potato, carrot, bell pepper, and onion, then stir-fry over medium-high heat for 4 minutes.*
❯ *Add remaining ingredients except lemon juice, garlic, and cilantro. Bring to boil. Cover and cook over medium-low heat for 1 hour or until meat and vegetables are well done. Stir in lemon juice, garlic, and cilantro, then serve.*

Uyghur Tomato and Cucumber Salad

Serves 4 to 6

1 large cucumber (about 8 inches), peeled and diced into ½-inch cubes

3 large firm tomatoes, diced into ½-inch cubes

1 small sweet onion, finely chopped

⅛ teaspoon cayenne pepper

1 tablespoon sugar

1 teaspoon salt

1 tablespoon olive oil

1 tablespoon white vinegar

2 tablespoons finely chopped fresh cilantro

❯ *Combine the cucumber, tomatoes, and onion in a salad bowl and set aside.*

❯ *In a small mixing bowl, stir together the cayenne pepper, sugar, salt, oil, and vinegar, then stir into the vegetables. Sprinkle cilantro over the salad and serve cold.*

Funchoza
Uyghur Noodle Salad

Serves 6

½ pound any type of rice noodles

½ pound lamb, cut into ½-inch cubes

4 tablespoons vegetable oil

1 medium onion, thinly sliced

2 medium carrots, cut in half lengthwise then very thinly sliced into half rounds

1 green bell pepper, seeded and cut into very thin slices

4 garlic cloves, crushed

3 tablespoons soy sauce

1 tablespoon white vinegar

1 cup stewed tomatoes

½ cup water

1 cup finely chopped fresh cilantro

½ teaspoon salt

1 teaspoon garam masala

1 small cucumber, sliced into rounds ⅛ inch thick

Packed full with flavors, *Funchoza* is a delicious stir-fry made with lamb, vegetables, and noodles. For the noodles, the rice variety are traditional, but they can be replaced with udon noodles or lo mein. This is simple to prepare and is a quick, nutritious dish.

❯ *Prepare noodles according to package instructions. Remove the cooked noodles and rinse in cold water, then cut the noodles into 4- to 6-inch pieces and set aside.*

❯ *Stir-fry lamb with oil for 5 minutes over medium-high heat. Stir in onion, carrots, bell pepper, garlic, soy sauce, and vinegar and continue stir-frying for 8 more minutes. Stir in remaining ingredients except cucumber. Stir in noodles, then transfer to serving dish. Decorate with the cucumber and serve.*

Polo — Uyghur Rice

Serves 4 to 6

5 tablespoons olive oil

½ pound lamb, cut into ½-inch cubes

1 small onion, finely chopped

2 medium carrots, julienned (about ⅛ inch thick)

1 garlic clove, crushed

3 cups water

1 teaspoon sugar

½ teaspoon salt

½ teaspoon ground cumin

⅛ teaspoon cayenne pepper

1 cup long-grain white rice, rinsed

4 tablespoons raisins

This simplified rice dish is served at weddings and other large gatherings.

❭ *In a saucepan, heat the oil, then sauté the lamb over medium heat for 7 minutes, stirring a number of times. Add the chopped onion and stir-fry until translucent (about 7 minutes). Stir in carrots, garlic, and water. Bring to boil, then cover and cook over medium-low heat for 20 minutes, stirring occasionally. Stir in sugar, salt, cumin, and cayenne pepper.*
❭ *Spoon and spread rice over the stew, but do not mix it with the rest of the ingredients. Spread the raisins evenly over the rice. Cover and cook over low heat for 20 minutes. Remove from heat and gently stir together the saucepan contents. Cover and let sit for 15 minutes.*
❭ *Transfer to a serving dish and serve immediately.*

Uyghur Spicy Lamb Kebabs

Serves about 4

1 small onion, chopped

4 garlic cloves

2 tablespoons olive oil

⅓ cup pomegranate juice

1 teaspoon salt

½ teaspoon black pepper

⅛ teaspoon cayenne pepper

1½ pounds lamb with some fat, cut into 1-inch cubes

There are innumerable ways in which the Uyghurs make their kebabs. This and the *Uyghur Cumin-Flavored Kebabs* (see below) are common ways in which they prepare this delicious dish.

❯ *Process onion and garlic in a food processor until they become a paste. Transfer to a bowl. Stir in remaining ingredients, except lamb, then thoroughly combine. Stir in lamb pieces, then cover and refrigerate and allow to marinate for 2 to 3 hours.*
❯ *Place lamb cubes on skewers and grill for about 8 minutes, turning them over several times and brushing with the marinade a few times. Serve hot with a salad.*

Uyghur Cumin-Flavored Kebabs

Serves about 4

1½ pounds lamb with some fat, cut into 1-inch cubes

Vegetable oil

2 teaspoons ground cumin

½ teaspoon ground coriander seeds

1 teaspoon salt

⅛ teaspoon cayenne pepper

This is a simpler type of kebab with a unique taste.

❯ *Place lamb cubes on skewers, then brush with oil.*
❯ *Combine remaining ingredients in a small bowl or cup. Sprinkle lamb cubes with the mixture. Grill for about 8 minutes, turning them over several times. Serve hot with a salad.*

Samsa — Meat "Hot Pockets"

Makes about 16

Dough:

1 (¼-ounce) package yeast

1 teaspoon sugar

¼ cup warm water

2 cups white flour

⅛ cup water

4 tablespoons butter, softened

½ teaspoon salt

Vegetable oil

Filling:

1 pound ground lamb (with some fat)

1 large onion, finely chopped

¾ teaspoon salt

½ teaspoon black pepper

½ teaspoon ground cumin

⅛ teaspoon cayenne pepper

2 tablespoons pomegranate syrup

1 tablespoon lemon juice

1 tablespoon olive oil

1 egg yolk, beaten

Samsa is a very typical Uyghur food, and they are traditionally baked in a special brick oven. These are delicious "hot pockets" stuffed with ground lamb, onions, and spices. The dough is very easy to make and serves as a light, crispy coating to the abundant stuffing.

To prepare dough:

〉 *Dissolve yeast and sugar in the ¼ cup warm water. Let stand for 10 minutes.*
〉 *Thoroughly combine the flour, the ⅛ cup of water, butter, ½ teaspoon salt, and the yeast mixture to form a smooth dough, adding a little water or flour if needed. Form the dough into a ball, then rub very lightly with a few drops of vegetable oil. Place in a bowl, then cover with towels and let it sit. Allow dough to rise for 2 hours.*

To prepare filling:

〉 *In the meantime, combine the filling ingredients.*

To assemble:

〉 *Preheat oven to 350° F.*
〉 *Form dough into large walnut-size balls, then cover and allow to stand for 30 minutes. With a rolling pin, roll out the balls into rounds 3 inches in diameter. Place a tablespoon of the filling in the middle of each round, then wet the inside edges of dough. Fold dough over the stuffing in a semicircle. Pleat and pinch the edges, then lift up edges of dough and twist to make the* **Samsa** *in the shape of a handbag. Place on a greased baking sheet. Brush with a bit of the egg yolk and bake for 30 minutes. Serve hot.*

Uyghur Nang Sweet Bread

Makes 10 small round loaves

1 (¼-ounce) package yeast

1 teaspoon sugar

¼ cup warm water

3⅛ cups white flour

1 cup water

¾ teaspoon salt

Sesame seeds

Sugar

Melted butter

The staple food of the Uyghurs, *nang* can be made with various flours, but the standard is wheat flour. Toppings include sesame seeds, onion, oil, butter, salt, some spices, and sugar, and it is usually served crispy—it's delicious! When served warm with honey and tea, it makes for a great breakfast or a tasty snack.

❯ *Dissolve yeast and sugar in the ¼ cup warm water. Let stand for 10 minutes.*
❯ *In a bowl, thoroughly combine the flour, the 1 cup water, dissolved yeast, and salt to form a smooth dough, adding a little water or flour if needed. Form the dough into a ball, then place in a bowl. Cover with towels and let sit in a warm place. Let rise for 1 to 2 hours or until it doubles in size.*
❯ *Form dough into 10 balls, then cover and allow to rise again for 30 minutes.*
❯ *Preheat oven to 500° F.*
❯ *Roll dough balls out into 8-inch rounds, then sprinkle lightly with sesame seeds and generously with sugar. Place on greased baking trays. Bake for about 6 minutes or until done. Sprinkle lightly with butter and serve immediately.*

Open-Faced Lamb Pies

Makes 12

Samsa dough recipe (see page 104)

1 pound ground lamb

1 medium onion, finely chopped

4 tablespoons pomegranate syrup

1 teaspoon salt

1 teaspoon garam masala

½ teaspoon black pepper

Yogurt

4 tablespoons finely chopped fresh mint leaves

These are very similar to the open-faced meat pies *(sfeeha)* found in the Greater Syria area—apparently a remnant from the trade on the Silk Road.

❭ *Prepare the* Samsa *dough following the same directions.*
❭ *While the dough is sitting, prepare topping by combining the remaining ingredients except the yogurt and mint. Set aside.*
❭ *When the dough has doubled in size, form into 12 balls. Roll out balls into 4-inch rounds and place rounds on oiled baking trays.*
❭ *Preheat oven to 350° F.*
❭ *Divide topping among rounds, pressing down to make a smooth and even topping.*
❭ *Bake uncovered for about 20 minutes or until they begin to brown.*
❭ *Drizzle with yogurt, garnish with the mint, and serve warm.*

Dapanji — Big Plate Chicken

Serves 8

1 package udon noodles

4 tablespoons cooking oil

2 pounds boneless chicken breast, cut into 1-inch cubes

1 teaspoon ground cumin

½ teaspoon black pepper

½ teaspoon ground aniseed

1 tablespoon grated fresh ginger

4 garlic cloves, crushed

1 medium onion, finely chopped

2 medium potatoes, peeled and diced into ½-inch cubes

1 medium bell pepper, seeded and diced into ½-inch squares

1 small fresh hot pepper, seeded and finely chopped

2 cups stewed tomatoes

¼ cup pomegranate juice

3 tablespoons soy sauce

2 teaspoons sugar

1 chicken bouillon cube, dissolved in 1 cup warm water

Cilantro, chopped

Traditionally this dish is made with cut-up chicken pieces, bone-in. However, I prefer making it with chicken breasts, as it is much easier to eat.

❯ *Prepare noodles as per instructions on package, then set aside but keep warm.*
❯ *Heat oil in a heavy frying pan or wok, then stir-fry chicken over medium-high heat for 5 minutes. Add the cumin, pepper, and aniseed, then stir-fry for a further 3 minutes. Add ginger, garlic, onion, potatoes, and sweet and hot peppers, then stir-fry for a further 3 minutes. Stir in tomatoes, pomegranate juice, soy sauce, sugar, and bouillon water. Bring to boil. Cover and simmer over medium-low heat for 40 minutes or until chicken and potatoes are well cooked.*
❯ *Divide the noodles into 8 serving bowls. Spoon the chicken stew on top and garnish with the cilantro before serving.*

CHAPTER 14

Kashmiri Wazwan

THE EPITOME OF FEASTS

The history of modern Kashmiri food can be traced back to Mongol Emperor Timur's savage invasion of India in the fifteenth century. With this invasion came a migration of skilled artisans from Samarkand to the Kashmiri Valley; among these were cooks trained in the cuisine of the courts. Called Wazas, the descendants of these cooks are still responsible for the banquet feasts called Wazwan, a ritual and ceremony for which Kashmir is noted.

Mutton and rice are the main ingredients in the diet of every Kashmiri. Some chicken and fish, as well as vegetables—dried in winter— are on the menu of that mountainous land. Yet by far the most important is sheep's meat. Almost every part of this animal is used in one dish or another.

For flavoring, aniseed, cardamom, chili flakes and powder, chiles, cinnamon, cloves, garlic, ginger, onions, saffron, tomatoes, yogurt, and the mouli flower (which lends color to food) are the most commonly used condiments. Mustard oil is often used for cooking. For dessert, semolina sweets are sometimes served after a Wazwan. Interestingly, the Kashmiri Brahmins who, unlike Brahmins in many parts of India, eat meat, keep away from two flavorings, garlic and onions, considering them aphrodisiacs.

Rich and redolent with the flavor of spices, Kashmiri food has developed a distinct personality of its own, unique to the Kashmir and Jammu regions in both India and Pakistan. Even though

their basic cuisine came with Timur's invasion, the Afghans, Arabs, Persians, and others have influenced it. In the past, the cooks in the Kashmiri Valley developed their banquets to become world famous. Almost every special occasion in Kashmir was celebrated with a Wazwan, considered to be the epitome of the Kashmiri culinary art—a cuisine that can match virtually any other cuisine in the world. Traditionally served at weddings and other important events, the feast is not simple to prepare and is quite costly. Considerable time and effort are invested in preparing a Wazwan. The feast takes days of planning and many hours of tedious preparation. The ultimate banquet is the Royal Wazwan, when master chefs traditionally offer thirty-six courses—all cooked under a master chef called Vasta Waza, assisted by an entourage of Wazas. Interestingly, all Vasta Wazas claim descent from the master chefs brought by Timur to the Kashmir Valley.

The Wazwan begins with the Vasta Waza and his helpers cutting, grating, and pounding the mutton, coaxing out of the meat numerous flavors and tastes. The Vasta Waza personally supervises and picks the ingredients to be used in each dish, ensuring that each dish is up to standard. When the many lamb and mutton dishes are all prepared, the feast begins—a vision of feasting in Paradise.

Based upon tradition, when a Wazwan commences, guests are grouped in fours and seated on the floor around a platter. Before the banquet feast begins, an attendant passes around tash-t-nari (jug and basin) with warm water that was heated in a samovar for the guests to wash their hands. Following the washing ritual, tramis (food platters) are put before the guests, one after the other. The first course is a large heaped platter of rice decorated with pieces of seekh kebabs, methis korma, tabak maaz, and sides of barbecued ribs. This is followed by trami after trami, ending with the dish gushtaba—for meat eaters, some of the most delicious food in the world.

Usually no more than one or two vegetarian dishes appear at a Wazwan. To serve all meat dishes is considered lavish hospitality; to serve more than two vegetarian dishes is considered inappropriate, indicating that the host was trying to economize. Chutney and curds are served separately in small clay pots. Only kahva (a green tea) is served to wash down the rich meal. At a traditional Wazwan, no forks or knives are ever used—food is eaten by hand.

The most formal of ceremonies in Kashmir, a Wazwan offers guests the best of all foods in the house—true hospitality usually much appreciated by those invited. Not a simple meal, but a colorful banquet featuring a series of gourmet meat delights, the feast is a memorable event in the lives of Kashmiris. Yet, sadly, except for some restaurants and a few Kashmiri homes in and out of the valley, the Wazwan has almost faded away—but not quite. Seven is the minimum number of dishes that can be served at a small Wazwan and this number is included in our mini Wazwan. I have simplified the following Wazwan dishes and have eliminated the tedious steps normally involved. Yet, served together, this little feast is fit for royalty, ready to serve an entourage of twelve guests.

Note: Since lamb is more readily available, I have used it to replace mutton, in the following recipes. In addition, I have replaced those spices and condiments that are not readily available with similar ingredients found in most supermarkets.

Seekh Kebabs

Serves 4 to 6

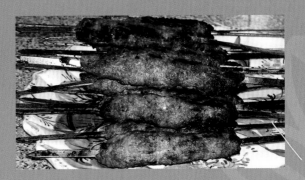

2 pounds ground lean lamb
1 medium onion, finely chopped
5 garlic cloves, crushed
1½ teaspoons salt
⅛ teaspoon ground cardamom
½ teaspoon ground ginger
½ teaspoon ground aniseed
½ teaspoon ground caraway
½ teaspoon dried, crushed mint leaves
¼ teaspoon chili flakes
2 tablespoons butter

Like all Muslim cooking in the Indian subcontinent and beyond, kebabs hold a high place in Kashmiri cuisine. They form part of almost all feasts and regular meals.

Process all ingredients in a food processor for about 2 minutes or until mixture is somewhat dough-like in consistency. Place on skewers, making each kebab from 6 to 8 inches long and 1 inch wide. Barbecue, turning them over until all sides are browned. Keep warm until ready to serve.

Paluo
Kashmiri Rice

6 tablespoons cooking oil

2 medium onions, finely chopped

2 tablespoons grated fresh ginger

1 teaspoon cumin seed

1 teaspoon ground turmeric

¼ teaspoon ground cardamom

2 cups long-grain white rice, rinsed

2 cups milk

2 cups water

1¼ teaspoons salt

4 tablespoons chopped toasted cashews

4 tablespoons chopped pistachios

½ cup raisins, rinsed

½ cup finely chopped fresh parsley

Heat the oil in a saucepan, then fry onions and ginger over medium heat for 6 minutes. Stir in cumin, turmeric, and cardamom, then stir-fry for a further 2 minutes. Stir in rice, milk, water, and salt, then bring to boil. Cover and cook for 15 minutes over medium-low heat, then stir in remaining ingredients and re-cover. Turn off the heat and let sit on the element for 30 minutes to allow to cook in its own steam.

Rogan Josh
Spiced Meat

3 tablespoons cooking oil

2 pounds lamb, cut into ½-inch cubes

⅛ teaspoon ground cloves

⅛ teaspoon ground cardamom

½ teaspoon cinnamon

½ teaspoon ground cumin

½ teaspoon chili flakes

1 cup plain yogurt

1 teaspoon salt

¼ teaspoon ground ginger

¼ teaspoon ground fennel seeds

¾ cup water

Usually found on a *Wazwan*, rogan josh is considered one of the top meat dishes in Kashmir. It is usually served with rice to important guests.

Heat oil in a saucepan, then stir-fry meat over medium heat for 5 minutes. Stir in cloves, cardamom, cinnamon, and cumin, then stir-fry for 10 minutes or until meat turns brown. Add chili flakes and yogurt, then stir-fry until the white of the yogurt disappears. Add remaining ingredients, then cover and cook over medium heat for 5 minutes. Serve hot.

ASIAN COOKING MADE SIMPLE

Rista — Meatballs with Gravy

2 pounds ground lamb

1½ teaspoons ground ginger

1¼ teaspoons ground aniseed

1½ teaspoons garam masala

1½ teaspoons salt

¾ teaspoon ground cardamom

4 tablespoons light sesame oil

6 garlic cloves, crushed

½ teaspoon black cumin seeds

6 cups water

½ teaspoon chili flakes

½ teaspoon turmeric

2 tablespoons dried onion flakes

¼ teaspoon cinnamon

Pinch saffron

This dish is excellent for an everyday meal when served with its gravy and rice or mashed potatoes.

❯ In a food processor, process lamb, 1 teaspoon of the ginger, 1 teaspoon of the aniseed, 1 teaspoon of the garam masala, 1 teaspoon of the salt, and ½ teaspoon of the cardamom for 2 minutes. Form into small, walnut-size balls, then set aside.

❯ To make the gravy, in a saucepan, heat oil, then add garlic and cumin seeds and stir-fry over medium heat until garlic begins to brown. Add water, chili flakes, turmeric, onion flakes, and remaining ginger, aniseed, and salt.

❯ Gently place meatballs in the pan with the gravy. Bring to boil, then cover and cook over medium-low heat for 50 minutes or until meatballs are well cooked. Add cinnamon, saffron, and the remaining garam masala and cardamom. Cook over medium-low heat for a further 10 minutes and serve hot with the gravy.

Muthi Kebabs

1½ pounds ground meat
½ cup very finely ground almonds
½ cup very finely ground roasted chickpeas
1 medium onion, chopped
2 garlic cloves, crushed
2 tablespoons plain yogurt
1 tablespoon pomegranate syrup
1 tablespoon finely chopped fresh mint leaves
1 tablespoon butter
1 teaspoon salt
½ teaspoon chili flakes
½ teaspoon allspice
½ teaspoon ground ginger
½ teaspoon ground coriander seeds
½ teaspoon black pepper

❯ *Preheat oven to 350° F.*
❯ *Process all ingredients in a food processor for 2 minutes or until contents are paste-like. Form into oblong kebabs, then bake in a pan for 50 minutes or until golden brown.*

Tabak Maaz
Fried Lamb Ribs

2 pounds lamb ribs (after most fat has been removed)
¾ cup milk, mixed with 1 cup water
4 garlic cloves, crushed
1 teaspoon ground ginger
1 teaspoon aniseed
1 teaspoon turmeric
1 teaspoon cinnamon
⅛ teaspoon ground cloves
1 teaspoon salt
8 cups water
½ cup butter

❯ *Cut ribs into pieces 5 to 6 inches long and 2 to 3 inches wide, making sure that there are 2 or 3 ribs in each piece.*
❯ *In a saucepan, stir all the ingredients except ribs and butter. Bring to boil. Add the ribs, then bring to boil and cover. Cook over medium-low heat for 1 hour or until the meat is tender, adding more water if necessary. Remove ribs with slotted spoon and set aside. Melt butter in a frying pan, then fry ribs over medium heat in two or more batches until they turn crispy and evenly browned. Keep warm until served.*

Aab Gosht — Lentil Stew

4 tablespoons cooking oil

2 large onions, finely chopped

1 pound lamb, cut into ½-inch cubes

3 medium tomatoes, finely chopped

4 garlic cloves, crushed

½ teaspoon ground ginger

¼ teaspoon chili flakes

½ teaspoon turmeric

1 teaspoon salt

½ teaspoon ground cumin

½ teaspoon ground coriander seeds

½ teaspoon black pepper

4 tablespoons finely chopped fresh cilantro

1 cup split lentils

2 cups coconut milk

3 cups water

2 fresh green chile peppers, seeded and sliced

Heat oil in a saucepan, then add onion and meat and cook over medium heat for 15 minutes, stir-frying every few minutes. Stir in tomatoes, garlic, ginger, chili flakes, turmeric, and salt, then simmer over medium-low heat for 15 minutes. Stir in cumin, ground coriander, pepper, cilantro, and lentils. Stir-fry for a few minutes. Add coconut milk and water, then bring to boil and cover. Cook over medium-low heat for 30 minutes or until meat and lentils are well cooked, stirring often and adding water if necessary to ensure that ingredients do not stick to the bottom of saucepan. Garnish with chile pepper, then serve hot.

Kahva — Kashmiri Tea

5 cups boiling water

1 tablespoon green tea leaves

4 cardamom pods, slightly split

1 cinnamon stick (about 1 inch long)

Fresh ginger, thinly sliced, about 1 x 1 inch

2 tablespoons sugar or according to taste

Place all ingredients, except sugar, in a saucepan. Bring to boil, then brew over medium-low heat for 3 minutes. Stir in sugar, then strain and serve.

Rava Kesari
Semolina Pudding

Serves 4

5 tablespoons butter

1 cup fine semolina

2 cups hot water

1¾ cups sugar

¼ teaspoon ground cardamom

⅛ teaspoon nutmeg

⅛ teaspoon ground cloves

Pinch saffron, dissolved in 1 tablespoon water

3 tablespoons raisins, soaked for 2 hours in hot water and drained

½ cup toasted cashew nuts, chopped

1 tablespoon pine nuts

Although not common, a semolina pudding sometimes follows the main courses of the *Wazwan*. It makes a fine end to the feast.

Melt butter in a frying pan, then stir-fry semolina over medium heat until it turns light brown. Gradually stir in the hot water. Stir continually for about 1 minute. Stir in sugar, cardamom, nutmeg, cloves, and dissolved saffron. Cook over medium heat, stirring continuously for 2 minutes and adding a little water if necessary. Stir in raisins and cashews, then place in serving cups. Decorate with pine nuts, then serve warm.

Gushtaba — Meatballs and Curds

2 pounds ground lamb

1½ teaspoons ground ginger

1¼ teaspoons ground aniseed

2 teaspoons salt

1½ teaspoons garam masala

¾ teaspoon ground cardamom

1½ cups plain yogurt

½ teaspoon chili flakes

½ teaspoon ground caraway seeds

4 tablespoons light sesame oil

⅛ teaspoon ground cloves

8 garlic cloves, crushed

4 tablespoons finely chopped fresh cilantro

2 tablespoons onion flakes

½ teaspoon black cumin seeds

½ teaspoon cinnamon

Gushtaba is called "dish of kings" by those who love it, and it is renowned for its flavor and taste. It is always served as the last dish in a Wazwan.

> *In a food processor, process lamb, 1 teaspoon of the ginger, 1 teaspoon of the aniseed, 1½ teaspoons of the salt, 1 teaspoon of the garam masala, and ½ teaspoon of the cardamom for 2 minutes. Form into walnut-size balls, then set aside.*
> *Process yogurt, chili flakes, and caraway in a food processor for 1 minute and set aside.*
> *Place meatballs in a saucepan, then cover with water. Add remaining ½ teaspoon of the ginger, ¼ teaspoon of the aniseed, and ½ teaspoon of the salt. Bring to boil, then cover and cook over medium heat for 50 minutes. Remove balls with a slotted spoon and place on a plate. Pour liquid into a bowl and allow to cool.*
> *Heat oil in another saucepan, then add cloves, garlic, the processed yogurt, and the meatball liquid. Stirring constantly, bring to boil over medium heat. Add the meatballs, cilantro, onion flakes, black cumin, cinnamon, and the remaining ½ teaspoon of garam masala and ¼ teaspoon of cardamom. Cover and cook over medium-low heat for a further 10 minutes. Serve meatballs in gravy, or remove meatballs and serve along with the gravy.*

CHAPTER 15

Hyderabad Cuisine

INDIA'S ROYAL FOOD

The city of Hyderabad, famous for its minarets and pearl bazaars, is the capital city of the state of Andhra Pradesh, a bustling 400-year-old metropolis of some 6 million people. Long renowned as the seat of the fabulously wealthy Nizams (rulers) who patronized expert artisans famous for piercing and stringing pearls, Hyderabad is a historic urban center that brings to mind romance and fabulous wealth. Like most of India's cities, it is a blend of fairytale and reality, a hodgepodge of old and new, forming an exotic background for its aristocratic cuisine. Asaf Jahi, one of the viceroys of the Mughal Empire in the sixteenth century, broke away to establish an independent state. Thereafter, his descendants gave themselves the title Nizam. In 1798, a military and political alliance was signed between the Nizam and the British, which continued until India became independent. During these centuries, the city developed a unique cultural and culinary heritage that remains well preserved. Today, the people of Hyderabad are noted for their culture, artistic abilities, and certain sophistication in manners. The fifth-largest cosmopolitan city in India, it is a city of oriental glory, reminiscent of the great days of Indo-Muslim culture. It is well known for its hospitality, and visitors to the city have always found a pleasant welcome there, as well as its fine food.

India's finest cuisine was developed from the fifteenth to the nineteenth centuries in the courts of the Mughal Emperors, who raised cooking to an art form. Today, in all parts of India and beyond, it is offered as a royal food. The rich cuisine of these refined aristocrats included a fusion of the indigenous culinary traditions, which had been nurtured for almost 3,000 years by the Vedic and Aryan people, with the foods of Arabia, Persia, Afghanistan, and the Turkic nations—later enhanced by including European touches.

Being an offshoot of the Mughals, the Nizams of Hyderabad were a party to this development of a fine distillation of taste. The Mughal court food and India's predominant Hindu culture formed the basis of the kitchen of the Nizams. This combination produced dishes that were to become the definitive in fine dining.

Even though vegetables are the king of foods in India, Mughal cuisine often includes goat and lamb, which are served as scrumptious kebabs, in curries, roasted, or barbecued. Even though India has had a series of movements to protect cows (which are sacred to Hindus), Hyderabad boasts of its delicious dishes of beef. Nevertheless, as a whole, other than lamb and chicken, Mughal food is mostly vegetarian, containing heavily spiced lentils, peas, and beans. Hyderabad is today famous for the distinctive aroma and taste of its biryani, a dish of rice and mutton or chicken. Travelers have written that in the past, a typical Hyderabadi feast would have no fewer than twenty-six different varieties of biryani, which has a reputation as an aphrodisiac. Perhaps equal to this rice dish in Hyderabadi homes is haleem, a dish especially popular during the holy month of Ramadan. A spicy flavored and savory dish of meat, wheat, and ghee cooked to a porridge-like consistency, its name literally means "patience" because it takes long hours to prepare. Among the hundreds of other Hyderabadi delicacies are kulcha, a soft leavened bread with a legend behind it that adds romance to its flavor; baghare baigan, a tasty eggplant dish; and sherwanis, pattar ka gosh, korma, pakodas, salans, tamatarkabkat, all with special enticing aromas and exotic flavors. Other favorites are vadas, delicious doughnut-shaped snacks dunked in steaming hot sambar (vegetable stew); deep-fried rice flour murku pastries; and steamed rice dumplings called idli. As a fitting end to the meal, one can savor payasam, a pudding made with rice and milk; kubani ke meetha, an apricot dessert served with whipped cream; almond-flavored badam kajali; sheer khurma, a delicacy of dry fruits and dates; an exotic range

of halwas; and the elaborately prepared paan.

Hyderabad's dedication to fine dining has been unwavering for many centuries, especially among the upper classes. Throughout the centuries, the Nizams of Hyderabad were famed for their sumptuous feasts and their love for fine dining; these centuries-old rich dishes are still cooked today.

Under the patronage of the Nizams, the cooks of Hyderabad devoted themselves to sharpening their culinary talents with the subtle blending of spices with emphasis on the fiery chile. In the process, they created an amazing range of superb dishes. Much to the delight of food lovers, one can today enjoy the unparalleled taste and flavor of the historic Hyderabadi creations thanks to these clever chefs.

In these samples of Hyderabadi dishes, I have simplified the recipes and substituted some ingredients that are hard to find. However, I have tried to maintain the same taste for all the recipes.

Double Ka Meetha
Bread Pudding

Serves 6 to 8

5 slices white bread, each slice cut into 4 pieces, then fried until golden

2 tablespoons lightly toasted chopped cashew nuts

3 tablespoons lightly toasted sliced almonds

½ cup sugar

¼ cup water

⅛ teaspoon ground cardamom

Pinch saffron, dissolved in 1 tablespoon water

½ cup hot milk

½ cup whipping cream

> *Arrange fried bread pieces in a large baking pan, then sprinkle with cashews and almonds. Set aside. In a saucepan, boil sugar and water, then cook for 5 minutes over low heat to make syrup, stirring a number of times. Stir in cardamom and saffron, then cook for a few more minutes.*
> *Spoon hot syrup evenly over nuts and bread, then pour milk evenly over top. Spoon cream over top, then refrigerate for a few hours before serving.*

Hyderabadi Bagare Baigan
Eggplant Curry

Serves about 6

1 eggplant (about 1½ pounds), peeled and cut into 8 to 12 slices
1½ teaspoons salt
½ cup vegetable oil
2 large onions, thinly sliced
2 tablespoons sesame powder
2 tablespoons coconut powder
2 tablespoons tamarind paste, dissolved in ½ cup water
1 tablespoon grated fresh ginger
2 fresh large chile peppers, seeded and finely chopped
4 garlic cloves, crushed
1 teaspoon ground cumin
1 teaspoon ground coriander seeds
1 teaspoon turmeric
1 teaspoon sugar
¼ teaspoon ground cloves
2 cups water
4 tablespoons finely chopped fresh cilantro

〉 *Sprinkle the eggplant slices with the salt, then set aside.*
〉 *Heat 2 tablespoons of the oil in a saucepan, then stir-fry onions until light brown, adding a little more oil if necessary. Stir in remaining ingredients except eggplant, water, and cilantro. Stir-fry for 2 minutes. Stir in water and boil uncovered over medium-high heat for 10 minutes.*
〉 *Heat the remaining oil in a frying pan, then fry eggplant pieces, a few at a time, over medium heat for about 10 minutes or until they begin to soften but are still firm, adding more oil if necessary. Remove and drain on paper towels.*
〉 *Add the fried eggplant to saucepan mixture. Reduce heat to medium-low and cook for a further 10 minutes. Decorate with the cilantro and serve with plain rice or Hyderabad-Style Biryani (see page 120).*

Hyderabadi Mirch Ka Salan
Fried Peppers

Serves about 6

6 tablespoons vegetable oil
2 medium onions, finely chopped
6 large sweet green peppers, seeded and cut lengthwise into strips ½ inch wide
1 fresh red chile pepper, seeded and finely chopped
1 teaspoon mustard seed
4 tablespoons ground sesame seeds
2 tablespoons unsweetened ground coconut
1½ teaspoons salt
1 teaspoon ground cumin
1 teaspoon black pepper
1 cup water
2 tablespoons lemon juice

Heat oil in a large frying pan, then fry onions over medium heat for 10 minutes. Add sweet and hot peppers and mustard seed, then stir-fry for 4 minutes. Stir in remaining ingredients except lemon juice. Cover and cook over medium-low heat for 10 minutes, stirring several times. Stir in lemon juice, then serve hot or cold.

Kalmi – Mung Bean Patties

Serves 4 to 6

1 cup mung beans, soaked overnight and drained
4 tablespoons white flour
1 large onion, chopped
2 fresh chile peppers, seeded and finely chopped
2 tablespoons grated fresh ginger
2 teaspoons baking powder
1 teaspoon salt
1 teaspoon ground coriander seeds
1 teaspoon ground cumin
1 teaspoon turmeric
½ teaspoon black pepper
1 egg, beaten
Oil for frying

❯ In a food processor, process all ingredients, except oil, into a smooth, soft paste, adding a little water if necessary.

❯ In a saucepan over medium heat, warm 1 inch of oil. Drop heaping tablespoons of the paste into the oil and deep-fry to golden brown. If patties tend to break, add more flour to the paste; if paste is too thick, add water. Drain on paper towels, then serve hot with chutney.

Dal Dhokli
Dumplings in Lentil Curry

Serves 6

1 cup lentils
4 tablespoons raw peanuts, chopped
8 cups water
3 tablespoons butter
6 garlic cloves, crushed
1 teaspoon cumin seeds
½ teaspoon mustard seed
1 teaspoon turmeric
1 teaspoon salt
⅛ teaspoon cayenne pepper
½ teaspoon ground coriander seeds
¼ teaspoon cinnamon
1 tablespoon sugar
½ pound white bread dough
2 tablespoons lemon juice
2 fresh green or red chile peppers, seeded and cut into thin slices
1 tablespoon finely chopped fresh cilantro

❯ In a saucepan, boil lentils, peanuts, and water. Cover and cook over medium heat for 1½ hours.

❯ Melt butter in a frying pan, then over high heat stir-fry garlic, cumin, and mustard seed for 3 minutes. Add frying pan contents, turmeric, salt, cayenne pepper, coriander, cinnamon, and sugar to lentils. Reduce heat to low and stir.

❯ Roll out bread dough to about ⅛ inch thick, then cut into 1-inch squares. Drop dough squares into the lentils, then cook for a further 15 minutes over medium-low heat, gently stirring a few times and adding more water if necessary. Stir in lemon juice, then transfer into a serving bowl. Garnish with fresh chiles and cilantro, then serve hot.

Hyderabad-Style Biryani

Serves 8 to 10

4 tablespoons olive oil

2 pounds lamb, cut into ½-inch cubes

2 medium onions, thinly sliced

Oil for deep-frying

1 tablespoon grated fresh ginger

1 teaspoon salt

1 teaspoon turmeric

⅛ teaspoon cayenne pepper

¼ teaspoon cinnamon

¼ teaspoon ground cloves

¼ teaspoon ground cardamom

1 cup plain yogurt

2 tablespoons lemon juice

4 tablespoons chopped fresh mint leaves

4 tablespoons finely chopped fresh cilantro

1 fresh small chile pepper, seeded and finely chopped

4 tablespoons cooking oil

3 cups long-grain white basmati rice, rinsed

10 cups water

⅛ teaspoon saffron

❯ Heat olive oil in frying pan over medium, then add lamb and fry for 10 minutes, stirring occasionally. Remove from heat and set aside.

❯ Deep-fry onions until golden. Drain on paper towels.

❯ Place lamb, ginger, salt, turmeric, cayenne pepper, cinnamon, cloves, and cardamom in a bowl, then thoroughly mix and let stand for 10 minutes. Add onions, yogurt, lemon juice, mint, cilantro, chile, and 2 tablespoons of the cooking oil, then mix and leave to marinate for 1 hour.

❯ Preheat oven to 350° F.

❯ In a saucepan, bring rice and water to boil. Cook over medium heat for 10 minutes, then drain, reserving 3 cups of the water. Place in a baking dish. Cover evenly with meat mixture, then sprinkle with remaining cooking oil. Mix reserved water with saffron, then pour evenly over top. Cover and bake for 1 hour. Serve hot.

Kubani Ka Meetha
Apricots with Whipped Cream

Serves 6

½ pound dried apricots, pitted

2 cups boiling water

4 tablespoons ground almonds

4 tablespoons sugar

¼ teaspoon almond extract

Whipped cream

❯ *In a saucepan, boil apricots and water. Cook over medium-low heat for 30 minutes, stirring occasionally.*

❯ *Mash apricots with their water, then return to saucepan and stir in almonds. Cook until mixture begins to thicken, then stir in sugar and almond extract and cook for a few minutes. Refrigerate, then serve with whipped cream.*

Chicken Pakodas

Serves 6 to 8

1 pound boneless chicken breast, cut into small pieces

2 eggs, beaten

1 cup white flour

4 teaspoons cornstarch

1 medium onion, finely chopped

½ cup chopped fresh cilantro

½ cup fresh mint leaves

1 tablespoon lemon juice

1 tablespoon hot chili sauce

1 tablespoon grated fresh ginger

2 teaspoons garlic powder

1 teaspoon turmeric

1 teaspoon salt

Oil for deep-frying

❯ *Place chicken in a saucepan and cover with water, then bring to boil. Cook for 1 hour over medium heat. Drain, reserving 1½ cups of the water, and let cool.*

❯ *Transfer chicken to a food processor, then add all other ingredients, except oil, and process for 2 minutes. Pour blend into a mixing bowl, then add enough of the reserved water to make a thick batter of dropping consistency, adding more water or flour if necessary. Heat oil in a saucepan, then drop in heaping tablespoons of batter. Remove when pakodas turn golden brown. Drain on paper towels. Serve with chutney or tomato ketchup.*

Lamb Korma

Serves 6

4 garlic cloves, crushed

1 tablespoon grated fresh ginger

2 cups water

4 tablespoons butter

2 pounds lamb, cut into 1-inch cubes

4 tablespoons vegetable oil

2 medium onions, finely chopped

2 tablespoons tomato paste, diluted in ¼ cup water

2 teaspoons ground coriander seeds

1 teaspoon turmeric

1 teaspoon ground cumin

1 cinnamon stick (about 4 inches long)

¼ teaspoon ground cloves

¼ teaspoon ground cardamom

¼ teaspoon cayenne pepper

1 teaspoon salt

½ cup plain yogurt

2 tablespoons lemon juice

❭ *Combine garlic, ginger, and water in a bowl, then set aside.*

❭ *Melt butter in a saucepan, then sauté lamb over medium heat until light brown. Stir in garlic, ginger, and water mixture, then cover and cook over medium-low heat for 40 minutes or until meat is well cooked, adding a little more water if necessary.*

❭ *In the meantime, heat oil in a frying pan, then sauté onions over medium heat for 10 minutes. Stir in remaining ingredients except yogurt and lemon juice. Stir-fry for 5 minutes. Transfer the frying pan contents to the saucepan, then stir in yogurt and lemon juice. Stir-fry for a few minutes and serve with cooked rice.*

Do Pyaxa — Hyderabadi Curry

Serves about 6

4 cups plain yogurt

4 medium onions (2 finely chopped and 2 thinly sliced)

1½ teaspoons ground coriander seeds

1½ teaspoons salt

2 pounds lamb, sliced into very thin pieces about 1 inch long

5 tablespoons butter

1 teaspoon ground cumin

1 teaspoon black pepper

¼ teaspoon cayenne pepper

1 teaspoon turmeric

> In a blender, blend 1 cup of the yogurt, the chopped onion, coriander, and salt for 1 minute. Transfer blender contents and meat into a bowl and thoroughly mix, then let stand for 1 hour.

> In the meantime, melt butter in a frying pan and fry sliced onions over medium heat until they begin to brown. Remove onions with slotted spoon and drain on paper towels. Reserve butter in frying pan and set aside.

> Mix fried onions with remaining 3 cups yogurt, then set aside.

> Re-heat butter, then add meat with its marinade as well as the cumin, pepper, and cayenne pepper. Cover and cook over medium-low heat for 20 minutes, stirring a few times and adding more butter if necessary.

> Preheat oven to 350° F.

> Transfer frying pan contents to a baking dish. Stir in yogurt-onion mixture and turmeric. Cover and bake for 40 minutes or until meat is well done. Serve hot from baking dish with cooked rice.

CHAPTER 16

Sri Lankan Cuisine

THE TASTE OF MANY NATIONS

Only separated from southeastern India by a 48-kilometers (30-miles) chain of shoals, the cuisine of the island of Sri Lanka (once called Ceylon by the British) has, through the centuries, been influenced by the dishes of the huge country to the north. The inhabitants of the country have to some extent modified these foods. Buddhists and Hindus created the vegetarian dishes, Christians remade the beef and pork recipes to their taste, and Muslims changed the lamb and mutton dishes to follow their own dietary rules.

Sri Lanka has for centuries been known for its spices. Thus, Sri Lankans use spices liberally in their cooking, giving the country's dishes extra tangs and aromas. To those not familiar with Sri Lankan food, this heavy use of condiments might make the dishes too spicy and hot. For those familiar with Indian curries, be forewarned that those of Sri Lanka are much hotter.

The best overall description of Sri Lankan food is "spicy-hot." Curry, which derives its name from the Tamil kari (sauce), forms the basis of most of the main dishes. The inhabitants are so enamored of the mixture of its spices that they have developed seventeen varieties of three main types, black, red, and white, each imbuing a subtly different taste to food. Curries are served with lunch, dinner, and, at times, breakfast. The bases of all curries are chiles, which are not native to the island. They were introduced into all of Asia from the New World by the Portuguese in the sixteenth century. The hot food of Asia that we know today did not exist before the colonization of the Americas.

Other invaders and traders also shaped the Sri Lankan kitchen. Arab and Malay traders, south Indian settlers, and Dutch and British invaders influenced the cuisine of the island. Lamprais, enjoyed in Sri Lanka today, are originally a Dutch recipe, while the British left their roast beef and roast chicken.

On the other hand, even though these introduced foods and the modern fast foods have their fans, the average Sri Lankan continues to relish traditionally hot, spicy dishes. Curry dishes are made from virtually every available fruit and vegetable, and from all types of chicken, fish, meat, and pulses (edible seeds).

Besides curries, boiled or steamed rice is almost always served as part of the main meal. It is eaten with a wide range of meats and vegetables.

Since Sri Lanka is an island, fishing has always been one of the main industries. The waters around the country teem with fish and other creatures of the sea, and these products are prepared in innumerable ways. One finds them almost always featured in daily meals, usually fresh. In addition, the countless fruits and vegetables grown on the island make Sri Lanka a haven for vegetarians.

To add extra flavor to numerous dishes, coconut milk is often used in the country's cooking. Even more distinctive to the country's dishes is the use of dried Maldives fish, imported from these Indian Ocean islands near Sri Lanka and used somewhat like shrimp paste as a taste enhancer in vegetable dishes. Its fans are convinced that this fish product increases the appetite.

A typical Sri Lankan meal includes a main curry dish, which could be beef, chicken, fish, lamb, or mutton, and several other curries such as lentil, eggplant, plus other vegetables as side dishes. Served alongside are condiments, chutneys, pickles, and samblos (a fiery paste).

Traditional desserts are common and numerous, from puddings and sweetmeats to rice and coconut-based desserts, as well as others based on fruit. Owing to its warm climate, Sri Lanka abounds in subtropical fruits, such as bananas, durians, jackfruit, mangoes, mangosteens, and rambutans.

Sri Lanka is famed for its tea, usually made with sugar and milk and, at times, with ginger. As for alcohol, Sri Lanka has two popular traditional beverages: a toddy derived from palm trees, and arrack, a refined form of toddy whose name comes from the Arabic name for an alcoholic drink, 'araq.

For those not accustomed to Sri Lankan food, be prepared to have your taste senses ignited. Be forewarned, but do not despair! A remedy for a burning mouth is to take a mouthful of noodles, rice, or yogurt—never water—to "cool things down."

In the following recipes, those spices or condiments that are hard to find have been replaced by similar ingredients, and the dishes have been modified in taste to appeal to the Western palate. Add more hot spices and they will become traditional Sri Lankan food.

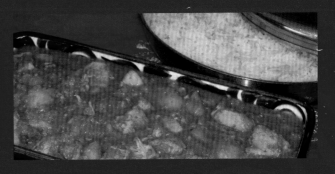

Chicken Curry

Serves 6 to 8

2 medium onions, finely chopped
4 garlic cloves, crushed
1 tablespoon grated fresh ginger
4 tablespoons vegetable oil
½ teaspoon cinnamon
½ teaspoon ground fennel seeds
4 cardamom pods
⅛ teaspoon ground cloves
1 tablespoon curry powder
2 pounds boneless chicken breasts, cut into 1-inch cubes
1 tablespoon tomato paste, dissolved in 1 cup water
1 large potato, peeled and cubed
1 teaspoon salt
½ cup thick coconut milk

〉 Process a third of the onions, half of the garlic, and the ginger in a food processor for 1 minute until mixture becomes a paste. Set aside.
〉 Heat the oil in a frying pan, then add cinnamon, fennel, cardamom, cloves, remaining onions, and remaining garlic. Sauté over medium-low heat for 6 minutes. Add the curry powder and continue sautéing for an additional 3 minutes. Add chicken, tomato paste, and the blended paste ingredients. Mix well until all the chicken pieces are coated. Cover and cook for 10 minutes over medium-low heat. Add potato and salt, then cover and simmer over medium-low heat for 40 minutes or until chicken and potato are well cooked, adding a little water if needed. Stir in the coconut milk, then cook for 4 minutes before serving, stirring a few times.

Sambol — Coconut Relish

Makes about 2¼ cup

2 cups desiccated coconut, mixed with ¼ cup warm water

1 small onion, chopped

2 garlic cloves, crushed

1 fresh medium red chile pepper, seeded

1 teaspoon salt

1 teaspoon paprika

2 teaspoons shrimp paste

2 tablespoons lemon juice

There are many types of sambol.
This is a simple type that is not too hot.

Process all ingredients in a food processor for 2 minutes, then serve with rice and curries.

Malu
Fish and Lentil Soup

Serves about 8

½ pound fish fillet, any kind of firm flesh fish, cut into 1-inch cubes

2 medium onions, finely chopped

½ cup split lentils

2 medium tomatoes, finely chopped

2 tablespoons finely chopped fresh cilantro

1½ teaspoons salt

1 teaspoon ground cumin

½ teaspoon black pepper

⅛ teaspoon cayenne pepper

6 cups water

2 tablespoons butter

1 tablespoon lemon juice

❯ *In a saucepan, boil fish, half of the onions, lentils, tomatoes, cilantro, salt, cumin, pepper, cayenne pepper, and water. Cover and cook over medium heat for 30 minutes.*
❯ *In the meantime, melt butter in a frying pan, then add the remaining onions and fry over medium heat for 10 minutes. Stir the onions into the soup and cover, then cook over medium-low heat for another 20 minutes. Stir in lemon juice and serve.*

Deep-Fried Shrimp Salad

Serves 4

Oil for deep-frying

1 pound shrimp, peeled and deveined

4 garlic cloves, crushed

1 tablespoon grated fresh ginger

1 teaspoon ground mustard seed

½ teaspoon salt

Pinch cayenne pepper

1 teaspoon sugar

4 tablespoons white vinegar

2 medium onions, thinly sliced

1 large sweet pepper, seeded and thinly sliced

> Deep-fry shrimp over medium-high heat for 3 minutes. Drain on paper towels and set aside.
> Place all ingredients, except shrimp, onions, and pepper, in a blender and blend for 1 minute. Transfer to a mixing bowl, then stir in remaining ingredients. Transfer to a serving platter and serve.

Eggplant Curry

Serves about 4

2 tablespoons vegetable oil

1 medium onion, finely chopped

4 garlic cloves, crushed

2 teaspoons curry powder

½ teaspoon chili flakes

1 teaspoon salt

½ teaspoon sugar

½ cup coconut milk

2 teaspoons white vinegar

1½ pounds eggplant, peeled and diced into 1-inch cubes, then deep-fried until golden

Heat oil in frying pan, then fry onion over medium-low heat for 10 minutes. Stir in garlic, curry powder, chili flakes, salt, and sugar and stir-fry for 1 minute. Add remaining ingredients, then reduce heat to low and simmer uncovered for 5 minutes, gently stirring a few times. Serve immediately.

Parippu Curry — Lentil Curry

Serves about 6

1 cup split lentils

1 fresh medium hot pepper, seeded and finely sliced

4 garlic cloves, crushed

½ teaspoon turmeric

1 tablespoon curry

3 cups water

1 cup coconut milk

1 teaspoon salt

4 tablespoons cooking oil

2 medium onions, finely chopped

1 teaspoon mustard seeds

⟩ *In a saucepan, boil together the lentils, hot pepper, garlic, turmeric, curry, and water. Cover and cook over low heat for 20 minutes or until lentils turn soft, stirring a few times and adding a little more water if necessary. Add coconut milk and salt, then cook over low heat for a further 10 minutes.*

⟩ *In the meantime, heat oil in a frying pan, then fry onions and mustard seed over medium heat for 10 minutes or until onions turn golden brown. Add frying pan contents into lentils, then cover and cook over low heat for 10 minutes, stirring a few times and adding a little water if necessary to keep somewhat mushy.*

Kiribath
Rice with Coconut Milk

Serves 4

1 cup short- or long-grain white rice, rinsed

1½ cups water

¼ teaspoon salt

1 cup coconut milk

Known as a festive dish, *kiribath* is usually served on holidays and feast days.

Boil the rice, water, and salt in a saucepan. Cover and cook over medium-low heat for 10 minutes or until the rice is soft and the water has been absorbed, stirring several times. Stir in coconut milk and bring to boil. Cook over medium heat until coconut milk is absorbed, constantly stirring. Spread on a platter, then refrigerate until cold. Cut into diamond shapes and serve.

Spinach and Lentil Curry

Serves 4 to 6

½ pound fresh spinach, thoroughly washed and chopped into small pieces

¾ cup split lentils

1 medium onion, finely chopped

2 garlic cloves, crushed

1 large sweet pepper, seeded and finely chopped

1 tablespoon curry powder

1 teaspoon turmeric

1 teaspoon ground mustard seed

1 teaspoon salt

3½ cups water

¾ cup coconut milk

In a saucepan, boil all ingredients except coconut milk. Cover and cook over medium-low heat for 40 minutes, stirring a few times and adding more water if necessary. Stir in coconut milk, then cook for a further 5 minutes before serving.

Kulfi
Sri Lankan Ice Cream

Serves 4 to 6

2 cups milk

1 cup sugar

2 tablespoons cornstarch

½ cup whipping cream

2 tablespoons chopped cashews

¼ teaspoon ground cardamom

In a saucepan, combine milk and sugar, then stir in cornstarch and bring to boil. Cook over medium heat for 10 minutes or until the saucepan contents thicken, stirring constantly, then remove from heat and stir in cream. Continue cooking and stirring for 5 minutes or until kulfi thickens somewhat. Pour into a serving bowl and allow to cool. Sprinkle with the cashews and cardamom, then refrigerate overnight before serving.

Rulang Aluwa
Semolina Squares

Makes 16 pieces

2 cups sugar

½ cup water

1 cup semolina or wheat hearts, lightly toasted

¼ teaspoon nutmeg

⅛ teaspoon ground cloves

½ cup chopped cashews

❯ *In a saucepan, mix together sugar and water and then cook for about 10 minutes or until syrup thickens, stirring often. Stir in remaining ingredients, then thoroughly mix. Pour mixture into a greased 8-inch square pan, then let cool.*
❯ *Cut into 2-inch squares and serve.*

CHAPTER 17

The Tasty Foods of Iran

ENSHRINED IN THE AURA OF HISTORY

When we cook with apricots, artichokes, eggplant, lemons, limes, oranges, pistachios, spinach, saffron, or tarragon, Iran should immediately come to mind. These cooking ingredients and many others came to us from that country, historically known as Persia. Its location at the very center of the Silk Road gave it a strategic position at a point of confluence between East and West in both the ancient and medieval worlds. This made it an ideal transition point for products being traded between the Orient and the West for thousands of years.

Many of these products were introduced into Iran from China and India in ancient times, then carried to the Iberian Peninsula by the Arabs after the rise of Islam. In the ensuing centuries, these products were spread from this once-Arab stronghold in Europe to the remainder of the continent. In many cases, the names of these food products and ingredients, in most European languages, still carry their Arabized-Persian names. As a few examples, in English, the apricot gets its name from the Arabic-Persian al-barquq; artichoke, al-khurshuf; lemon and lime, laymun; orange, naranj; and spinach, isbanakh.

The Iranian use of seasoning in their food goes back to the beginning of civilization. Continuing the Sumerian and Babylonian culinary tradition of using condiments in Mesopotamia, the cuisine of Iran developed into the haute culture of kings. Tablets from the time of these ancient peoples indicate that the inhabitants of Mesopotamia were using basil, cilantro, cumin, and caraway in their food some 4,000 years before the birth

of Christ. Over time, the culinary art of Iran was refined by the use of these and a good number of other local herbs and spices, as well as the introduction of plants and products from neighboring lands. Through the centuries, they were able to develop an exquisite cuisine by using just the right amount of seasoning in their combination of spices and herbs.

Onions and garlic are used only in small amounts, it is said, in order not to offend others. Cinnamon, cardamom, cloves, coriander, dill, nutmeg, paprika, pomegranates, saffron, sumac, turmeric, as well as orange-flower water and rose water, are added with discretion, not to overpower, but only to enhance the main ingredients. A whole world of sweet and sour sauces, stuffed vegetables, and greens such as grape leaves, and countless types of pastries were developed. Meat and fruit are often cooked together and enhanced by the minimal use of herbs and spices to form exotic dishes. A balance between sweetness and tartness is always kept by the subtle use of fresh and dried fruits. It is no wonder that, for hundreds of years, Iran has boasted one of the most sophisticated kitchens in western Asia. Many of the staples of Iran, including wheat bread, eggplant, chickpeas, dried fava beans, lamb, lentils, rice, and yogurt are also embedded in the foods of the Middle East. However, Iran carries its art of cooking one step further. Iranians consume rice much more than the other people in that part of the world. Rice is served at almost every meal. At the pinnacle of the rice dishes is chelo koresh (crusty baked rice topped by a sauce), which is served in most households at least once daily.

Second to rice is the use of wheat and its products. Both cooked, cracked wheat (bulgur) and rice are served boiled, steamed, or in pilaf. With respect to meat, Iranians prefer young, tender lamb and, to a lesser extent, goat. Generally, meats are combined with rice in dishes such as tah chin (layered rice, yogurt, and lamb) or the many dolmeh (stuffed vegetable) dishes. To a lesser extent are beef, chicken, and fish featured as main ingredients.

Some well-known Iranian dishes are abgousht (a meat and vegetable stew); fesenjan (chicken in pomegranate and walnut sauce); and shirin polo (chicken breast with rice and sliced almonds.) The crown jewel of the Iranian national cuisine, chelo kebab (marinated charcoal-grilled lamb served over rice), is considered the top dish of the country. Grilled tomatoes, naan (a pita-like bread), and panir (a feta-like white cheese) are usually served with chelo kebab.

Although in the Western world Iranian food is usually associated with kebabs, Iranian cuisine also includes a wide variety of cheeses, eggs, dairy, grains, legumes, vegetables, yogurt, and fruit. Whole, ground, or chopped nuts, especially pistachios, walnuts, and almonds, are also extensively used as ingredients or to decorate a good number of foods. Sabzi khordan (fresh herbs served with bread, cheese, cucumber, and walnuts), kuku (egg and vegetable cakes), aash (a series of soups), maast-o-khiar (cucumber in yogurt), and especially eggplant (called the potato of Iran) are popular dishes enjoyed by all.

Iranian cuisine is well noted for its forty-some types of bread in all shapes and forms. Some type of flat bread is always served with every meal.

The usual desserts are fresh fruits. However, there are also countless pastries, like baklava, as well as shirinis (puddings), candied and dried fruits, nuts, raisins, and honey, all served with a sweet drink called sharbat. Tea, rather than coffee, is the national beverage. Sweet hot tea (herbal and regular) is the usual refreshment, served in tiny cups and enjoyed at the beginning of the day, at breaks during work, and to accompany social or business engagements. On the other hand, almost as important in the daily life of the Iranians is dugh (yogurt diluted with water and lightly salted). Refreshing and delightful, it is served as a drink, usually accompanying meals. From Iran's historic kitchen, I have taken a few traditional dishes and simplified and adapted them to my taste. I have tried to keep their essence and culinary attributes intact.

Chelo Kebabs
Kebabs with Rice

Serves 6

2 pounds tender beef steak, cut into strips about 3 x 1½ x ½ inch

2 medium onions, grated or processed in a food processor for 1 minute

4 tablespoons olive oil

1½ teaspoons salt

½ teaspoon black pepper

3 tablespoons melted butter

12 small tomatoes, halved and sprinkled with salt and pepper

> Combine meat, onions, olive oil, salt, and pepper, then refrigerate for 3 to 4 hours to marinate.
> Place meat on skewers, then grill until done, brushing occasionally with butter. Place tomatoes on skewers and grill separately, then serve both together, placing meat and tomatoes over a platter of rice.

Abgousht — Beef Stew

Serves 6 to 8

1 cup dried chickpeas, soaked overnight in water with ½ teaspoon baking soda

½ cup white beans, soaked overnight in water with ¼ teaspoon baking soda

½ pound beef, cut into ½-inch cubes

1 large onion, finely chopped

1 fresh small hot pepper, seeded and finely chopped

4 tablespoons finely chopped fresh cilantro

2 teaspoons salt

1 teaspoon turmeric

½ teaspoon black pepper

½ teaspoon ground cumin

12 cups water

1 large tomato, chopped

1 large potato, peeled and diced

¼ cup long-grain white rice, rinsed

4 tablespoons lemon juice

Croutons

Drain chickpeas and beans, then place in a saucepan along with beef, onion, hot pepper, cilantro, salt, turmeric, pepper, cumin, and water. Bring to boil, cover, and cook over medium-low heat for about 2 hours until the chickpeas and beans are well cooked. Add tomato, potato, and rice, then cook over low heat for another hour or until all ingredients are very well cooked, stirring often and adding more water if necessary. Strain out the solids, then return juice to heat, adding water to make 6 to 8 servings. Stir in lemon juice, then heat and keep hot. Finely mash solids in a serving bowl, then serve as an entrée. Serve the juice in a separate bowl as a soup. Let diners add croutons to taste.

Khoresh Bamieh
Okra Stew

Serves 6

4 tablespoons butter

1 pound lamb, cut into ½-inch cubes

1 medium onion, finely chopped

2 garlic cloves, crushed

1 fresh small hot pepper, seeded and finely chopped

2 cups stewed tomatoes

2½ cups water

1 teaspoon turmeric

1 teaspoon salt

½ teaspoon black pepper

½ teaspoon ground cumin

1 pound frozen okra, thawed

Melt butter in a saucepan, then add lamb and sauté over medium heat for 10 minutes. Add onion, garlic, and hot pepper, then sauté for a further 10 minutes, stirring a few times. Add tomatoes and water, then bring to boil. Cover and cook over medium heat for 30 minutes. Stir in remaining ingredients except okra. Once saucepan contents are mixed well, gently stir in okra and bring to boil. Re-cover, then simmer over medium-low heat for 30 minutes, adding a little more water if necessary. Serve hot with cooked rice.

Maast-o-Khiar
Cucumber in Yogurt

Serves 4

2 cups plain yogurt

1 small cucumber (about 5 inches), finely chopped

½ cup finely chopped green onion

2 tablespoons finely chopped fresh mint leaves

1 tablespoon finely chopped fresh cilantro

½ teaspoon salt

½ teaspoon black pepper

1 clove garlic, crushed

Thoroughly mix all ingredients in a serving bowl. Refrigerate for 2 to 3 hours, then serve.

Kubideh Kebabs
Ground Meat Kebabs

Serves 6

2 pounds lamb with a little fat, ground or processed until very smooth

2 medium onions, grated

2 eggs, beaten

1 tablespoon lemon juice

1 teaspoon salt

½ teaspoon black pepper

½ teaspoon turmeric

½ teaspoon ground cumin

½ teaspoon cinnamon

½ teaspoon dried thyme

3 tablespoons melted butter

12 small tomatoes, halved and sprinkled with salt and pepper

> *Mix all ingredients, except butter, until sticky. Divide into about 20 balls, then mold each ball around a skewer until shaped like a large cigar about 1½ inches thick. Grill for a few minutes on each side, brushing occasionally with butter, until done.*
> *Place tomatoes on skewers and grill separately, then serve both together, placing kebabs and tomatoes over a platter of rice.*

Chicken Kebabs

Serves 6

2 pounds boneless chicken breast, cut into 1½-inch cubes

2 medium onions, grated

4 tablespoons lemon juice

1½ teaspoons salt

1 teaspoon black pepper

1 teaspoon marjoram

⅛ teaspoon saffron, diluted in 2 tablespoons water

3 tablespoons melted butter

12 small tomatoes, halved and sprinkled with salt and pepper

There is nothing better than tender and moist seasoned chicken fresh off the grill. Marinating the chicken in the morning lends to the infusion of flavors by the time it is ready to serve at dinner.

> *Place chicken, onions, lemon juice, salt, pepper, marjoram, and saffron in a bowl, refrigerate and allow to marinate for 6 to 8 hours. Place chicken on skewers, then grill, brushing occasionally with butter, until cooked.*
> *Place tomatoes on skewers and grill separately, then serve both together, placing kebabs and tomatoes over a platter of rice.*

Fesenjan
Chicken in Pomegranate Sauce

Serves 6

1 small eggplant (about 1 pound)

2 teaspoons salt

4 tablespoons butter

1 medium onion, chopped

1 pound boneless chicken breast, cut into ½-inch cubes

1 cup chopped walnuts

3 cups hot water

3 tablespoons pomegranate syrup

1 teaspoon black pepper

1 teaspoon turmeric

6 tablespoons cooking oil

¼ teaspoon ground cardamom

> *Peel eggplant and cut into pieces about 3 inches long and ¼ inch thick. Sprinkle ½ teaspoon of the salt over pieces. Place in a sieve, topped with a heavy weight for 1 hour to drain water.*
> *Melt butter in a saucepan, then add onion and sauté over medium heat for 8 minutes. Stir in chicken and stir-fry for 4 minutes, then stir in walnuts and stir-fry for another 2 minutes.*
> *Add water, pomegranate syrup, remaining salt, pepper, and turmeric, then bring to boil. Cover and simmer over low heat for 30 minutes.*
> *In the meantime, heat oil in a frying pan, then sauté eggplant until the pieces just begin to brown, adding more oil if necessary. Place eggplant on top of chicken, then simmer over low heat for 20 minutes, adding a little water if necessary. Stir in cardamom, then cook for 5 minutes longer. Serve with cooked rice.*

Dolmeh-yeh Barg-e Mow — Stuffed Grape Leaves

Serves about 6

1 pound jar grape leaves or fresh grape leaves

1 pound lamb, ground or cut into very small pieces

1 cup long-grain white rice, rinsed

2 medium onions, very finely chopped

2 medium tomatoes, finely chopped

4 garlic cloves, crushed

½ cup finely chopped green onion

2 tablespoons finely chopped cilantro

4 tablespoons olive oil

1 teaspoon sugar

1 teaspoon black pepper

½ teaspoon ground cumin

½ teaspoon allspice

2 teaspoons salt

2 cups tomato juice, mixed with 1 teaspoon dried oregano

> If using grape leaves in jar, unroll and thoroughly wash out salt from leaves. Cover with boiling water and let stand for 30 minutes, then drain. If using fresh grape leaves, dip the leaves in boiling water, then drain.

> Prepare stuffing by combining all remaining ingredients except 1 teaspoon of the salt and the 2 cups tomato juice.

> Place approximately 1 heaping tablespoon of stuffing, depending on leaf size, on wide end of each leaf. Roll the leaf tightly, making sure to tuck in ends when rolling. Continue until all leaves are rolled or all stuffing is used.

> Place any extra leaves on bottom of a saucepan. Arrange rolls tightly side by side in circular layer on bottom of saucepan. For the next layer, repeat the same process but arrange rolls in alternate direction. Continue process until all rolls have been layered. Sprinkle remaining salt over top, then pour tomato juice over rolls. Cover with inverted plate, then add enough water to barely cover plate. Bring to boil, then cover. Cook over medium-low heat for 1 hour or until meat and rice are done. Serve hot.

Kukuye Sabzi — Omelet

Serves 4

5 eggs, beaten
1 medium onion, finely chopped
1 tablespoon white flour
1 cup finely chopped green onion
1 cup finely chopped fresh parsley
½ cup finely chopped fresh dill
½ cup finely chopped fresh cilantro
¼ teaspoon salt
¼ teaspoon black pepper
¼ teaspoon ground cumin
¼ teaspoon turmeric
4 tablespoons butter

› *Preheat oven to 350° F.*
› *Thoroughly combine eggs with remaining ingredients except butter. Set aside.*
› *Melt butter in an 8-inch round baking dish, then pour in egg mixture. Cover and bake for 25 minutes. Cut omelet into 4 wedge-shaped pieces, then turn each piece over. Return to oven and bake for a further 10 minutes or until golden brown. Serve hot or cold.*

Chelo Seebzamini — Iranian Rice

Serves 6

8 cups water
2 cups long-grain white basmati rice, thoroughly rinsed and drained
1¼ teaspoons salt
¼ teaspoon crumbled saffron threads, diluted in 2 tablespoons hot water
¼ teaspoon sugar
6 tablespoons butter, melted
1 medium potato, peeled and thinly sliced

› *Boil water, rice, and 1 teaspoon of the salt in a saucepan. Cover and cook over medium-low heat for 8 minutes, stirring a number of times. Drain in a sieve. In the meantime, combine saffron, sugar, 2 tablespoons of the butter, and remaining ¼ teaspoon of salt in a bowl. Add potato slices and turn them with a fork until they are thoroughly coated. Transfer to and spread coated potatoes to cover the bottom of a baking dish, then set aside.*
› *Preheat oven to 350° F.*
› *Stir 2 tablespoons of the butter into the rice, then spread rice evenly on top of potatoes. Sprinkle remaining 2 tablespoons butter on top, then cover and bake for 50 minutes. Bottom of potatoes will brown.*
› *Place rice in a mound on a serving platter, and then arrange potato slices (browned side up) on the rice. Serve with all types of stews and barbecued meats.*

Zoolbiya — Lattice-Shaped Fritters

Makes about 18 fritters

Syrup:

2 cups sugar

1 cup water

3 tablespoons liquid honey

¼ teaspoon saffron, diluted in 2 tablespoons boiling water

2 tablespoons lemon juice

3 teaspoons rose water

Batter:

1 (¼-ounce) package yeast

1 teaspoon sugar

1¼ cups warm water

1 cup white flour

¾ cup cornstarch

⅛ teaspoon salt

1 egg white, beaten until stiff

Light olive oil or vegetable oil for deep-frying

One of the most popular sweets in Iran, it is also a well-known fritter in India, the Middle East and North Africa. Crispy, light, and sweet, it has stood the test of centuries. This is my version of this fritter.

To make syrup:

In a saucepan, stir together the sugar and water, then stir in the honey and diluted saffron. Over medium heat, bring to boil, then simmer for 12 minutes over medium-low heat. Stir in lemon juice and simmer for 2 minutes. Stir in rose water and simmer for 1 minute. Remove from heat and let cool.

To make batter:

> *Dissolve yeast and sugar in ¼ cup of the warm water. Let stand for 10 minutes.*
> *In a mixing bowl, add the flour, cornstarch, and salt and mix well. Form a well and add the yeast, the remaining 1 cup warm water, and the egg white. Beat with an electric mixer for 1 minute to make the batter smooth. Cover the bowl and let sit for 1 hour to allow the batter to rise. After it has risen, stir.*

> *In a deep saucepan, heat the oil over medium heat. Using a funnel, place a finger under the opening and spoon 3 tablespoons of batter into the top of the funnel. Placing the funnel over the saucepan, remove the finger from the opening and dribble the batter quickly into the oil by moving the funnel rapidly over the surface, creating a lattice form. Fry on both sides until golden. Remove from oil, gently shaking to remove excess oil. Immerse in the syrup, making sure to cover both sides. Place on a serving platter.*

CHAPTER 18

The Foods of Iraq

A TREASURE OF HISTORY

Iraqi cuisine has a long history, going back some 10,000 years to the Sumerians, Akkadians, Babylonians, Assyrians, and ancient Persians. Tablets found in the ruins left by these ancient peoples show recipes prepared in the temples during religious festivals—these being the first known cookbooks in the world. Iraq, the Mesopotamian cradle of the ancients, was home to many dazzling and sophisticated civilizations, highly advanced in all fields of knowledge, including the culinary arts.

However, it was in the medieval era, when Baghdad was the capital of a large Muslim empire, that the Iraqi kitchen reached its zenith. After the destruction of Baghdad by the Mongols in A.D. 1258, this world-class cuisine declined, but was somewhat revived in the twentieth century by the commercial and cultural interaction with the countries of the Mediterranean area and the world beyond. Today, the foods of Iraq reflect this rich inheritance as well as strong influences from the culinary traditions of Ottoman Turkey and Iran and the Greater Syria area. Because of all these traditions and complex influences, Iraqi cuisine is enormously rich and varied.

As in the other countries of the Middle East, chicken and especially lamb are the favorite meats. Because of the consumption of lamb and other meat, Iraqi cuisine is rich in protein and iron. With the exception of most appetizers and salads, regular daily dishes are usually based on red meat, in many cases marinated with garlic,

lemon, and spices, then grilled over charcoal. Although the grilling of kebab (skewered chunks of lamb or chicken) is preferred, quzi (grilled whole lamb stuffed with rice, almonds, raisins, and spices) and kubba (minced meat ground with bulgur or rice and spices) are close runners-up. Unlike the neighboring Arab countries, Iraqis add raisins and other fruits to their stuffing for fowls. Stuffed vegetables such as dolma are favorites, as is rice. Hardly any meal is served without rice, usually the basmati variety grown in the marshes south of Baghdad. Butter and yogurt are other essentials in Iraqi cooking. Often food is prepared with butter, and yogurt is consumed with the main meal as a drink or sauce, or just as a side dish. Bulgur (cooked, dried, then crushed wheat) has been a staple in the country since the days of the ancient Assyrians.

The most renowned dish in Iraq is masgouf (an Iraqi grilled fish specialty). It is simply a fish, opened flat, spiced with salt, pepper, and tamarind, then placed on wooden sticks and barbecued in front of a large flame. It is usually served with rice cooked with tomato paste or saffron, along with salad and pickles. However, in the last few decades masgouf has become extremely expensive, making it a dish only for special occasions.

For enhancing the food, Iraqis often use baharat, a mixture of spices usually including cinnamon, cloves, nutmeg, cumin, coriander seeds, and paprika. This combination of spices, as well as the amount used, may vary somewhat from region to region. As a rule, Iraqi cuisine is not overly spicy.

Most meals are accompanied by samoons, a type of Iraqi bread. Samoons also serve as great snacks when accompanied with a variety of appetizers such as cheese, olives, and jams. Served almost daily are fresh vegetables and fruits, especially the renowned Iraqi dates. These are sweet and very delicious, and they are served with coffee at the end of almost every meal.

Due to the different climatic zones of Iraq, the country produces a great variety of fruit. In the north, with its cold winter weather, apples, pears, peaches, plums, and all types of nuts thrive; in the hot and humid south, a rich variety of dates (some 120 kinds) flourish; and in the hot and dry center, some of the world's best and sweetest melons are grown. Even though most of the dishes served in big-city restaurants present standard Middle Eastern and international foods, Iraq's style of cooking is distinctive. The country's food is milder and less spicy than some neighboring countries, and its non-Arab neighbors have influenced more of its dishes.

These few dishes in a minuscule way tell the story of a cuisine as old as time. I have prepared them to my taste, so they are spicier than the regular Iraqi dishes.

Kabab Iroog — Meat Kebabs

Depending on size, makes 20 to 25 kebabs

1 pound ground lamb or beef

½ cup dried fine bread crumbs

1 small sweet pepper, seeded and finely chopped

1 large tomato, finely chopped

1 medium onion, chopped

2 garlic cloves, crushed

2 tablespoons chopped fresh cilantro

½ cup white flour

1 egg, beaten

1 teaspoon salt

½ teaspoon black pepper

½ teaspoon ground cumin

½ teaspoon turmeric

Unlike in other Middle Eastern countries where kebabs are usually barbecued, traditional Iraqi kebabs are made into patties and fried. I have tried them both fried and baked in an oven, and I found the oven kebabs preferable. Also, I have added an egg, an ingredient not traditionally part of the *Kabab Iroog* recipe. The egg helps to bind the kebab.

❭ *Preheat oven to 350° F.*
❭ *Mix meat and bread crumbs together in a bowl.*
❭ *Process sweet pepper, tomato, onion, garlic, and cilantro in a food processor for 1 to 2 minutes.*
❭ *Combine processor contents with meat mixture, mixing well. Add the remaining ingredients and mix well.*
❭ *Form into patties about ½ inch thick. Place patties on a greased baking pan. Bake for 1 hour or until golden brown on top.*

Labna
Yogurt Cheese Balls

Serves 4

4 cups yogurt

¼ lemon rind, finely grated

1 teaspoon lemon juice

1 teaspoon salt

¼ teaspoon dried mint

¼ teaspoon dried thyme

Olive oil

This basic cheese, as old as time, is a great breakfast dish, especially when served with Arab (pita) bread.

› *Thoroughly mix all ingredients, except olive oil, then place in a cloth bag and hang over a sink or another vessel to catch the liquid. Allow to drip for 4 days at room temperature.*
› *Form cheese into balls a little smaller than walnuts, then place in a jar. Pour in enough olive oil to cover, then store and use as needed.*

Eggplant and Laban (Yogurt)

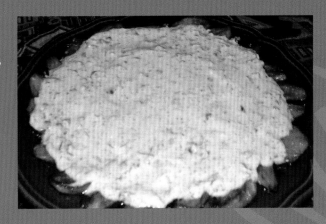

Serves about 6

1 medium eggplant (about 1 pound)

1 teaspoon salt

½ cup vegetable oil

1 cup plain yogurt

2 tablespoons finely chopped fresh cilantro

4 garlic cloves, crushed

½ teaspoon black pepper

½ teaspoon ground cumin

› *Peel eggplant, then cut in half and slice lengthwise into slices ¼ inch thick. Place on a platter and sprinkle with ½ teaspoon of the salt and set aside.*
› *Heat the oil in a frying pan, then fry eggplant until lightly golden, turning slices over once, adding more oil if necessary. Drain on paper towels, then arrange on a serving platter.*
› *Thoroughly mix remaining ingredients, including remaining salt, then pour evenly over eggplant slices and serve.*

Tepsi Baytinijan — Meat and Vegetable Casserole

Serves about 6

1 eggplant (about 1 pound)

2 teaspoons salt

½ cup vegetable oil

3 medium carrots, peeled, then cut into ½-inch-thick round slices (3 medium potatoes may be substituted)

2 medium onions, cut into ½-inch-thick round slices

1 pound ground lamb or beef

4 garlic cloves, crushed

1 teaspoon black pepper

1 teaspoon ground cumin

⅛ teaspoon cayenne pepper

½ cup water

3 medium tomatoes, cut into ½-inch-thick round slices

❯ Peel eggplant, then halve lengthwise and slice into half rounds about 1 inch thick. Place on a platter and sprinkle with ½ teaspoon of the salt and set aside.

❯ Heat oil in a frying pan, then fry eggplant slices over medium heat for about 6 minutes, turning over once, or until light golden, adding more oil if necessary. Drain on paper towels.

❯ In the same oil, adding more oil if necessary, lightly fry the carrots and onions over medium heat for 10 minutes, stirring occasionally, then set aside. Drain carrots and onions on paper towels. Put frying pan with its oil aside.

❯ Thoroughly combine meat, half the garlic, ½ teaspoon of the salt, ½ teaspoon of the pepper, ½ teaspoon of the cumin, and cayenne pepper, then form into small balls. Fry in same frying pan over medium heat for 10 minutes, adding more oil if necessary and stirring occasionally, then set aside.

❯ Combine water, the remaining salt, garlic, pepper, and cumin, then set aside. Preheat oven to 350° F.

❯ Arrange the eggplant pieces on the bottom of a baking dish. On top of the eggplant, evenly arrange carrots, onions, and slices of tomatoes, in that order. Spread meatballs evenly atop the tomato slices, then pour water mixture on top.

❯ Cover and bake for 1 hour, then serve hot from the baking dish.

Jajeek — Yogurt and Cucumber

Serves 4

2 cups plain yogurt

1 cucumber (about 6 inches long), finely chopped

2 garlic cloves, crushed

2 tablespoons olive oil

2 tablespoons finely chopped fresh mint leaves

½ teaspoon salt

¼ teaspoon black pepper

This is a simple appetizer common in the Middle East. In Iraq it is usually served as an appetizer but can also be served as a salad.

Thoroughly combine all ingredients, then chill and serve.

Sumac Salad

Serves 4 to 6

2 medium cucumbers (about 6 to 7 inches long), quartered lengthwise, then thinly sliced

1 large tomato, quartered, then sliced ¼ inch thick

1 medium sweet onion, cut in half and very thinly sliced

3 tablespoons olive oil

2 tablespoons sumac

¾ teaspoon salt

½ teaspoon black pepper

Probably one of the most commonly used condiments in the Middle East, sumac is a tangy spice that enhances the flavor of foods without overpowering them. It is a good replacement for lemon juice and even salt. Some believe that the dish of lentils served by Jacob to Esau was spiced with sumac. In later centuries, the Greek physician Dioscorides (A.D. 40–90) mentions sumac in his writings. The Romans used it in a number of their dishes but for some unknown reason, in the ensuing centuries its use never caught on in the countries of the West.

❯ *Place cucumber, tomato, and onion in a salad bowl and combine, then stir in remaining ingredients and serve.*

Kubbat Ruzz — Rice Kubba

Makes about 20 kubbas

3 tablespoons butter

2 pounds ground lamb or beef

3 tablespoons pine nuts or chopped walnuts

1 medium onion, finely chopped

2½ teaspoons salt

1¼ teaspoons black pepper

¾ teaspoon allspice

¼ teaspoon nutmeg

3 cups cooked long-grain white rice

½ cup white flour

2 tablespoons olive oil

1 teaspoon ground cumin

¼ teaspoon cayenne pepper

This *kubba*, a favorite in Iraq but made a little more spicy than in other Middle Eastern countries, is one of the *few kubbas* that does not include bulgur as a main ingredient.

> In a frying pan, melt butter over medium heat, then sauté ½ pound of the meat until it begins to brown. Stir in pine nuts or walnuts, onion, ½ teaspoon of the salt, ¼ teaspoon of the pepper, ¼ teaspoon of the allspice, and nutmeg, then sauté until onion is limp, about 8 minutes. Set aside for use as stuffing.

> Process rice in a food processor until dough-like. Add remaining meat, salt, pepper, allspice, as well as the flour, olive oil, cumin, and cayenne pepper. Process until a smooth dough is formed, adding a little flour or water if necessary. Form a golf-ball-size piece of kubbat ruzz dough. While holding ball of dough in one hand, use the forefinger of the other hand to press a hole and begin expanding the hole by rotating and pressing against palm of hand until you form an oval shell of ¼ inch thickness. Place a heaping tablespoon of stuffing into the hollow shell. Close the shell, then form into an egg-like shape. (Use cold water on hands to help shape and close shells.)

> In a saucepan, heat oil over medium heat, then deep-fry in oil, turning kubba until golden brown. Drain on paper towels. Serve hot.

Shawrabat Laban Barida
Cold Yogurt and Cucumber Soup

Serves 6 to 8

5 cups plain yogurt
1 cucumber (about 6 inches long) peeled and finely chopped
2 cups water
6 tablespoons finely chopped fresh cilantro
½ cup almonds, pulverized
2 teaspoons salt
¾ teaspoon black pepper
⅛ teaspoon cayenne pepper

Thoroughly mix all ingredients in a serving bowl, then chill for at least 2 hours before serving.

Shawrabat 'Adas
Lentil Soup

Serves 6 to 8

1 cup dry split lentils

8 cups water

4 tablespoons cooking oil

1 large onion, finely chopped

½ pound ground lamb or beef

2 garlic cloves, crushed

2½ teaspoons salt

1½ teaspoons black pepper

1 teaspoon ground coriander seeds

4 tablespoons butter

1 teaspoon ground cumin

½ teaspoon turmeric

2 tablespoons lemon juice

Lentil soup, often served during Ramadan (the Muslim holy month of fasting), is also very popular throughout the country at any time of the year.

❯ *Place lentils and water in a saucepan and bring to boil, then cover and cook over medium heat for 40 minutes or until lentils turn mushy.*
❯ *Heat oil in a frying pan, then sauté onion over medium heat until golden brown and set aside.*
❯ *In a mixing bowl, thoroughly combine meat, garlic, ½ teaspoon of the salt, ½ teaspoon of the pepper, and ½ teaspoon of the coriander. Form into marble-size balls.*
❯ *Heat butter in frying pan, then fry meatballs until golden brown on all sides.*
❯ *Stir into the lentils the onion, meatballs, cumin, turmeric, the remaining 2 teaspoons of salt, 1 teaspoon of pepper, and ½ teaspoon of coriander. Cover and cook over medium heat for a further 10 minutes, adding more water if necessary. Stir in lemon juice and serve.*

Klaycha — Date Cookies

1 pound soft dates, pitted and finely chopped

½ cup butter

½ teaspoon ground cardamom

¼ teaspoon ground cloves

2 cups white flour

⅓ cup sugar

1 teaspoon baking powder

½ teaspoon salt

½ cup shortening

⅓ cup milk

This is one of Iraq's famous sweets, and it has a history that goes back to the days of the ancient Mesopotamian civilizations.

> *In a saucepan over low heat, cook dates, butter, cardamom, and cloves. Stir occasionally until dates become a paste. Remove from the heat, then allow to thoroughly cool.*
> *In the meantime, combine flour, sugar, baking powder, and salt in a mixing bowl. Form a well in the mixture and add shortening and milk. Knead into dough, adding more milk if necessary, then divide into 4 parts. Roll out one at a time until about ¼ inch thick.*
> *Preheat oven to 325° F.*
> *Divide date paste into 4 parts, then roll out between 2 sheets of plastic the same size as the dough. Remove plastic, then place date layer on dough. Roll into a cylinder shape, jellyroll style. Continue process with the remaining 3 parts of dough. Slice rolls into 1-inch pieces, then place on a greased baking tray.*
> *Bake for about 25 minutes or until klaycha begin to turn golden brown. Allow to cool before placing on serving platter.*

CHAPTER 19

Foods of the Arabian Gulf Countries

For untold centuries, the Bedouins of the Arabian Peninsula have served honored guests mansaf (roasted lamb with rice) in their desert tents. Along the eastern coast of that ancient land, the inhabitants have, through the ages, adapted this traditional symbol of Arab hospitality. They add many more spices to the rice, and often serve fish instead of lamb, along with side dishes.

As has been the custom for hundreds of years, the lamb or fish and the rice are served together on a single brass or copper tray. This is then placed in the center of the circle of seated guests, within reach of all the diners. The piping hot meat atop a mountain of rice releases an enticing aroma, a prelude to what they are about to eat.

The age-old etiquette of the meal begins with the ritual washing of the hands. The diners then commence by tearing bite-size pieces of meat or fish with the fingers of the right hand. With the same hand, the pieces of meat or fish are rolled into the rice then squeezed by the same hand into a ball and tossed into the mouth. Everyone eats in silence, as if the food has a hypnotizing effect. When the meal is finished, hands are washed again and the guests are served coffee and, at times, sweets. Now everyone takes part in lively conversation while some smoke the traditional water pipes.

In all the Arab lands, traditional dining has moved today from the desert to elegant villas and plush city restaurants. However, mansaf remains a universal favorite, as popular with foreigners as with the local population. Western visitors are usually offered their meals on tables, with plates, knives, forks, and china, while Arab guests are served their food on a cloth spread over a carpet on the floor. Arab hospitality ensures that visitors from every part of the world will feast in comfort.

No traveler should leave the Arabian Gulf countries without trying a typical mansaf. The subtle flavor of the rice engulfing the lamb or fish with the aroma of herbs and spices ensures that it will be a memorable meal. Those who are privileged to sit down to such a feast will not quickly forget their Arabian sojourn.

In the past, the simple foods of Bedouins and pearl divers dominated the Arabian Gulf countries' cuisine. The choice of ingredients was limited, basically consisting of seafood and rice brought by Arab dhows (sailing ships) that traded along the coasts of East Africa and the Indian subcontinent. However, as centuries rolled by, these renowned ships of commerce brought back with them the spices of India and of the Indonesian archipelago. Subsequently, the people of the Gulf began to develop their own types of tasty foods, dominated by the aromatic smells of these spices.

The perfumes emanating from these spices gave a soft touch to the once harsh life lived by most of the people of the Gulf area. Afnan R. Zayani, in her book A Taste of the Arabian Gulf, writes: "In those days, women would daily decorate their simple homes with fragrant flowers and constantly burn oud (incense). This love for aromatic smells found its way to their taste in food to the extent of using the word khaneen—meaning perfumed—to pay a compliment to a particularly delicious dish."

The Arab connection with spices goes back a long way. For centuries, even before the birth of Christ, Arab merchants controlled the spice trade. Acting as middlemen, they transported exotic herbs and spices to the Mediterranean region and beyond. This continued until the Portuguese in the sixteenth century captured the Arab-controlled ports and trade routes.

The Arab hold on not only the spice trade but all commerce was so strong that in the medieval ages, Arabic was considered to be the language of traders. When Columbus attempted to reach India by sailing westward, he took an Arabic-speaking interpreter with him because Europeans in that era believed that Arabic was the only trading language in the world.

In addition to the spice trade, in the past few decades the newly discovered oil wealth in the Arabian Gulf countries has enticed millions of workers from around the world. This has been instrumental in adding new foods to the time-honored mansaf.

Today, a wide variety of side dishes are offered along with lamb or fish. The Gulf's link to the Indian subcontinent, going back for thousands of years, has imparted the taste of India and Pakistan to many of these foods. This, added to the Iranian and the influences of the neighboring Arab lands, has created a world of gourmet dishes in the kitchens of the Arabian Gulf countries.

The following dishes are some samples of these foods, which have taken on many of the spices from the Indian subcontinent. I have prepared them to my taste, either adding or changing spices.

Al-Dukous
Baked Tomatoes

Serves 6 to 8

4 large tomatoes (about 2 pounds), sliced about ¼ inch thick

4 tablespoons olive oil

6 garlic cloves, crushed

4 tablespoons finely chopped fresh cilantro

1½ teaspoons salt

1 teaspoon paprika

½ teaspoon black pepper

½ teaspoon ground cumin

¼ teaspoon cayenne pepper

❯ Preheat oven to 350° F.
❯ Place tomato slices in a baking dish, then set aside.
❯ Combine remaining ingredients, then spread evenly over tomato slices. Cover and bake for 25 minutes, then serve hot from baking dish with all types of meats.

Qahwa
Arabian Cardamom Coffee

Serves 10

3 tablespoons unroasted coffee beans

4½ cups water

1½ teaspoon pulverized cardamom seeds

The traditional way of roasting coffee beans was over an open fire. However, the old way has now been replaced by electric and gas stoves. Cardamom coffee may seem a little unusual when first sipped, but the taste catches on quickly.

> Place coffee in a heavy frying pan, then roast over high heat, stirring constantly until it just begins to brown. Remove and allow to cool. Coarsely grind.
> Boil water in a medium saucepan. Add coffee, then boil over medium heat for 10 minutes. Add cardamom, then boil for 5 minutes. Remove saucepan from heat and cover to let coffee grounds settle for 1 minute. Pour through a sieve into an ibriq *(coffee serving pot)* or a carafe. Steep for 5 minutes. Pour into demitasse cups and serve.

Kabab Alnikhi
Chickpea Kebabs

Makes about 36 patties

1 can chickpeas, drained

1 medium onion, chopped

1 medium tomato, chopped

½ cup fresh or frozen green peas

½ small sweet green pepper, seeded and chopped

1 teaspoon baking powder

½ cup white flour

1½ teaspoons salt

1 teaspoon ground cumin

1 teaspoon ground coriander seeds

1 teaspoon black pepper

2 tablespoons finely chopped fresh cilantro

2 eggs

Oil for frying

Like numerous other dishes now common in the Arabian Gulf countries, this dish likely came from the Indian subcontinent. Wholesome and tasty, it can be served as an entrée, side dish, or as a snack.

In a food processor, process all ingredients, except oil, until they become a soft dough (soft enough for spooning), adding a little water or more flour if necessary. Make sure that chickpeas are well ground. Pour oil in a saucepan to about 1½ inches deep, then heat over medium. Spoon dough by heaping tablespoon into the oil. Fry until golden brown, turning kebabs over once. If kebabs break up in the oil, add more eggs or flour to the dough. Continue until all the dough is finished. Drain on paper towels, then serve warm.

Nashab — Nut Rolls

Makes 72 to 88 pieces, depending on number of phyllo sheets in package

Syrup:

2 cups sugar

1 cup water

2 tablespoons lemon juice

Filling:

1¼ cups raw cashews

1 cup walnuts

½ cup blanched almonds

1 teaspoon ground cardamom

1 cup sugar

1-pound package phyllo dough

Oil for deep-frying

These sweets have a history that goes back to eighth-century Baghdad, when the city was the cultural and commercial center of the world. *Lawzinaj*, a phyllo pastry stuffed with ground almonds and sugar and one of the more luxurious sweets of that time, most likely is the forerunner of the Gulf's *nashab* rolls.

To make the syrup:
In a saucepan, mix together the sugar and the water and bring to boil. Simmer over low heat for 10 minutes. Stir in lemon juice and simmer for 5 minutes. Remove from heat and allow to cool.

To make the filling:
Process cashews, walnuts, almonds, cardamom, and the sugar in a food processor for 1 minute. Set aside.

> *Cut phyllo dough into quarters, then cover with a slightly damp cloth. Take one piece at a time and place 1 level tablespoon of filling along the middle of bottom edge. Fold both sides over filling. Slightly dampen top edge, then roll from bottom up. Repeat until all phyllo dough pieces are finished.*
> *Pour oil in a saucepan to 1 to 2 inches deep, then heat. Deep-fry rolls over medium heat, turning them over until they evenly turn golden. Remove rolls, then place in syrup for a few moments. Remove from syrup and allow to cool.*

Dukous Badhinjan
Eggplant Puree

Serves 8 to 10

1 large eggplant (about 2 pounds),
pierced in a few places with a fork

⅓ cup tahini

⅓ cup lemon juice

4 tablespoons olive oil

2 garlic cloves, crushed

1½ teaspoons salt

½ teaspoon black pepper

½ teaspoon ground cumin

⅛ teaspoon cayenne pepper

1 tablespoon pomegranate seeds

Fresh parsley leaves

For all strata of society in the Arab countries, eggplant is a favorite vegetable. This dish is prepared almost the same as in the eastern Arab countries—but with more spices in the Gulf countries.

❯ *Preheat oven to 350° F.*
❯ *Roast eggplant until skin blackens and becomes crisp, about 1 hour. Remove from the oven, then allow to cool.*
❯ *Remove eggplant skin, then place eggplant in a food processor. Add remaining ingredients, except pomegranate seeds and parsley, then process into a paste. Spread on a flat serving platter, then decorate with pomegranate seeds and parsley. Serve hot or cold.*

Shawrbat Alnikhi
Chickpea and Tomato Soup

Serves 8 to 10

1 cup dried chickpeas, soaked overnight and drained

8 cups water

4 tablespoons olive oil

4 tablespoons finely chopped fresh cilantro

2 medium onions, chopped

4 garlic cloves, crushed

2 cups stewed tomatoes

1½ teaspoons salt

1 teaspoon ground cumin

½ teaspoon black pepper

½ teaspoon turmeric

⅛ teaspoon cayenne pepper

❯ *Boil chickpeas and water in a saucepan. Cook over medium heat for about 2 hours or until chickpeas are well cooked, adding more water if necessary.*
❯ *In the meantime, heat oil in a frying pan, then sauté cilantro and onion over medium heat for 10 minutes. Stir in remaining ingredients and cook for a further 5 minutes.*
❯ *Add frying pan contents to the chickpeas. Cover and cook over medium heat for 20 minutes, then remove from heat and allow to cool. Puree, then return to saucepan, adding more water if desired. Heat and serve.*

Coconut Rolled Stuffed Dates

1 pound pitted whole dates (deglet or medjool)

½ cup coarsely chopped walnuts

¾ cup half-and-half

⅔ cup sugar

1 tablespoon orange blossom water

4 tablespoons cocoa

1 cup shredded coconut, spread on a dish

❯ *Slit dates on one side, then stuff with walnuts. Press closed, then set aside.*
❯ *To make the cocoa syrup, boil half-and-half in a small pot. Add sugar, then stir over medium heat until it dissolves. Add orange blossom water and cocoa, then, stirring constantly, cook over medium-low heat for 5 minutes. Remove from heat and allow to cool.*
❯ *Dip dates in the cocoa syrup, then roll them in coconut and place on a serving tray.*

Rubiyan — Shrimp and Rice

Serves 6 to 8

8 tablespoons butter

1½ pounds fresh or frozen shrimp, thawed, peeled, and deveined

4 garlic cloves, crushed

2 medium onions, finely chopped

2 cups long-grain white rice, rinsed

1 teaspoon salt

½ teaspoon black pepper

½ teaspoon cinnamon

½ teaspoon ground coriander seeds

¼ teaspoon cayenne pepper

4 cups water

Easy to prepare as the main course for special dinners, this dish and Makbous Samak (see page 153) are very tasty, especially for those who are looking for different fish menus.

❯ *Melt butter in a saucepan, then sauté shrimp with garlic over medium-low heat for 5 minutes or until shrimp turn light pink. Remove shrimp, but reserve butter. Chop half of shrimp into small pieces. Set aside separately chopped and unchopped shrimp and keep warm.*
❯ *In same butter, sauté onions over medium heat for 10 minutes. Add rice, then stir-fry for 1 minute. Stir in chopped shrimp and remaining ingredients except the whole shrimp. Bring to boil. Cover, then cook over medium-low heat for 20 minutes, stirring a few times and re-covering. Turn heat off, then stir and re-cover. Let stand for another 30 minutes on element to allow rice to cook in its own steam. Transfer to a serving platter and spread the remaining whole shrimp evenly over top. Serve hot.*

Salatat Khiyar
Cucumber Salad

Serves 6 to 8

4 tablespoons olive oil
1 large onion, finely chopped
1 medium sweet pepper, seeded and finely chopped
1 teaspoon ground ginger
¾ teaspoon salt
2 cups yogurt
2 medium cucumbers, peeled and chopped

Heat oil in a frying pan, then sauté onion and sweet pepper until onion turns limp, but not brown. Transfer frying pan contents into a serving bowl and allow to cool. Stir in remaining ingredients, then refrigerate for at least 1 hour. Serve chilled.

Makbous Samak
Lentils, Rice, and Fish

Serves 8 to 10

6 tablespoons butter
2 cups long-grain white rice, rinsed
½ cup lentils, soaked overnight in 5½ cups water
½ teaspoon black pepper
½ teaspoon ground cumin
½ teaspoon ground ginger
⅛ teaspoon cayenne pepper
2½ teaspoons salt
½ cup olive oil
4 medium onions, finely chopped
4 pounds fish fillet, cut into 2-inch cubes
1 teaspoon garlic powder

› *Melt butter in a saucepan, then add rice and stir-fry for 1 minute. Add lentils with their water, pepper, cumin, ginger, cayenne pepper, and 1 teaspoon of the salt. Bring to boil, then cover. Cook over medium-low heat for 20 minutes, stirring a few times and re-covering. Turn heat off, then stir and re-cover. Let stand on element to cook in its own steam for another 30 minutes.*
› *In the meantime, heat 4 tablespoons of oil in a frying pan, then sauté onions over medium heat until they turn golden brown. Set aside, but keep warm.*
› *Place fish fillets on a platter, then sprinkle with remaining salt and garlic powder. Heat remaining oil in a frying pan, then fry fillets over medium heat for about 10 minutes, turning them over a few times. Do not over-cook. Set aside, but keep warm.*
› *Place rice and lentils on a platter, then spread onions evenly over top. Arrange fillet pieces over onions and serve.*

CHAPTER 20

The Exotic Cuisine of Yemen

THE ANCIENT "ARABIA FELIX"

"I've been invited to an authentic Yemeni feast!" Excitement gripped me as I told my friend in Sana'a, Yemen's capital, that at last I was going to sample the country's cuisine at its best. My appetite had been whetted a long time before when I had read that Ibn Rusta, an Arab traveler who visited Sana'a in the tenth century, had written in his Book of Useful Notes that the city was unrivaled in its many tasty foods. At last, I was to test his culinary observation.

Detroit, Michigan, has a large Yemeni community. A former Yemeni consul stationed there had invited us for a magnificent meal his family was preparing for business colleagues and friends. Knowing that my brother and I were planning to visit Sana'a with a group of American Yemeni immigrants, he had included us with his other guests. His hospitality is very common in modern Yemen. It is said that in the remote districts of the country, a Yemeni farmer or tribesman will shoot over the heads of travelers if they pass without stopping to sample his hospitality.

When we arrived, a cover had been spread on the carpeted floor, with cushions all around. Plates and bowls of attractively laid-out foods covered every inch of space. Now I thought of Ibn Rusta's words as our host and about fifty guests, including a number of visiting foreign women (Yemeni women do not usually dine with strangers) sat on the floor around the steaming dishes. With us were high government officials and company executives who, along with peasants and workers, continue to eat in the ways of their ancestors. Yemenis, even affluent merchants and the highly educated, have not followed the Western trend. They continue to sit on the floor and eat by hand.

Silently we dipped our right hands (which we had previously washed in an adjoining room) into the savory foods. The enticing aromas floated around us as we feasted on the foods of this ancient land whence hailed the Queen of Sheba. It seemed that we were living in one of the stories of the Arabian Nights.

The origin of Yemeni cuisine goes back to the ancient civilizations of Awsan, Hadramout, Ma'in, and Qataban, and the two important powers in the ancient world, Saba and Himyar. Controlling the rich trade in frankincense, myrrh, and the spices that were brought from India and beyond to be sold to the kingdoms of the north, these South Arabian countries prospered. Through the years, a number of the condiments in which these South Arabians traded entered their culinary arts, and they developed a tasty cuisine.

Cardamom, caraway, coriander seed, cumin, fenugreek, saffron, turmeric, and, after the discovery of the Americas, fiery chiles became the preference in flavorings. Yemenis love hot, spicy foods prepared with these seasonings. They also love garlic and a good number of herbs, especially fresh cilantro and mint leaves. Fenugreek is the most commonly used spice, forming the basis of an everyday paste-sauce called hulba.

It goes well with zhug, a similar food enhancer. These accompany all meals and are added to almost every non-sweet dish.

Yemenis have always been great meat consumers. However, during the many centuries when the Imam rulers kept the country in a medieval state and most of the people were poor, meat, along with eggs and milk, were the food of the upper classes. Today, all this has changed. Due to the discovery of oil and many of the peasants emigrating, then returning with money, these foods have become common through most strata of society.

Chicken, beef, and the most popular, lamb, are grilled or boiled. Nothing is wasted. Water from the boiled meat and stock made from boiling the bones is used in preparing soups, or spiced and served as a watery broth. For those who can afford it, meat is served daily.

Even without meat, the simple diet of the poorer classes is nourishing and healthy. Bulgur, leafy greens, dried beans, lentils, rice, eggplant, okra, tomatoes, and sorghum, along with a number of other cereals, form the bulk of the ingredients in daily meals, always accompanied by bread served hot from the oven. Very little fat is used in cooking. It is not surprising, then, that the country has a good record when it comes to few heart ailments.

Along the country's long coastline, fish is more often part of meals. Honey, believed to increase sexual prowess, has, since time immemorial, been popular among rich and poor alike. For tartness, lemon is always used, never vinegar. Coffee, from the Arabic qahwa, is served to end the meal. Strange as it may seem in the land where coffee was first drunk, it is not brewed from the beans but from the husks, and it is served strong and very sweet with ginger.

To appreciate the cuisine of Sheba's land, one must dine in a Yemeni home. Tearing succulent pieces of meat by hand, then washing them down with warm bread dipped in one of the sauces, was for me an exotic way of enjoying the foods of this ancient part of the world. Nonetheless, if a visit to Yemen seems to be relegated to another time or another life, do not despair. These few dishes will give an insight into the culinary delight of a country that the Romans called "Arabia Felix" or, rather, "Happy Arabia."

Zhug — Spicy Relish

Makes about 1 cup

1 small (6-ounce) can tomato paste

6 garlic cloves, crushed

1 teaspoon salt

1 teaspoon black pepper

1 teaspoon crushed caraway seed

1 teaspoon crushed coriander seeds

1 teaspoon crushed cardamom seeds

½ teaspoon cayenne pepper

This relish adds a hot and spicy flavor to all types of Yemeni foods.

Thoroughly combine all ingredients, then refrigerate and use as needed.

Hulba
Fenugreek Paste

Makes 1½ to 2 cups

2 tablespoons ground fenugreek

1½ cups water

Yemenis use *Hulba* flavored with *Zhug* (see page 155) as a dressing for salads and as a sauce for meats, vegetables, and other foods, or as a dip.

Mix ingredients in a bowl. Let stand for at least 2 hours. Drain, then, adding a little water at a time, stir until bubbly. Refrigerate and use as needed. Should be used within 1 week.

Salta — Ground Meat Stew

Serves 8

4 tablespoons olive oil

1 pound ground beef or lamb

2 medium onions, finely chopped

4 medium potatoes, peeled, then diced into ½-inch cubes

2 medium tomatoes, finely chopped

1 teaspoon salt

½ teaspoon black pepper

5 cups beef broth

2 eggs, beaten

2 tablespoons finely chopped fresh cilantro

2 tablespoons *Zhug* (see page 155)

2 tablespoons *Hulba* (see above)

Salta is one of the main dishes in Sana'a and is considered Yemen's national dish.

Heat oil in a 3-quart saucepan, then sauté meat and onions over medium heat for 10 minutes, stirring a number of times. Add potatoes, tomatoes, salt, pepper, and broth, then bring to boil. Cover and cook over medium-low heat for 1 hour or until meat and potatoes are well cooked, adding more water if necessary. Stir in eggs and cilantro, then cook for a further 2 minutes. Remove from heat, then stir in Zhug and Hulba and serve immediately.

Fatut
Scrambled Eggs and Bread

Serves 4 to 6

4 tablespoons butter

2 cups small pieces of Arab bread (pita)

5 eggs, beaten with 2 teaspoons *Zhug* (see page 155)
and 1 teaspoon *Hulba* (see page 156)

⅛ teaspoon salt

Fatut is normally served with fresh bread right out of the oven. There is nothing tastier than a spicy wake-up meal.

Melt butter in a frying pan, then stir-fry bread pieces until they begin to brown. Pour egg mixture over bread. Stir for a few minutes until eggs are cooked. Serve hot.

Yemeni Bean Salad

Serves about 8

2 cups dry broad beans (fava beans), rinsed and soaked overnight and drained

6 tablespoons lemon juice

4 tablespoons olive oil

2 tablespoons tahini

2 teaspoons salt

½ teaspoon black pepper

⅛ teaspoon cayenne pepper

4 hard-boiled eggs, chopped

4 tablespoons finely chopped fresh cilantro

> *Place broad beans in a saucepan and cover with water to about 2 inches above the beans. Bring to boil, then reduce heat to medium and cook until beans are tender, but not soft enough to break up. Add more water if necessary. Drain, transfer to a mixing bowl, and allow to cool.*
> *In the meantime, combine the lemon juice, olive oil, tahini, salt, pepper, and cayenne pepper. Stir into beans, then add half of the chopped eggs and gently toss. Place on a serving platter. Garnish with remainder of eggs and cilantro, then serve.*

Bint Al-Sahn — Honey Cake

Makes 2 (9-inch) pies

1 (¼-ounce) package yeast

¼ cup warm water

1 teaspoon sugar

2¼ cups white flour

½ teaspoon salt

3 eggs, beaten

¼ cup whole milk

¾ cup butter, melted

½ cup liquid honey

Always served as a first course on special occasions, *Bint al-Sahn* (meaning "the girl of the dish") can also be eaten with the meal. However, it makes an excellent breakfast dish or a fine dessert.

❭ *In a bowl, dissolve yeast in water and stir in sugar. Cover and let stand for 10 minutes.*
❭ *In a mixing bowl, thoroughly combine flour and salt, then set aside.*
❭ *In another bowl, combine dissolved yeast, eggs, and milk, then slowly add flour and knead into a sticky dough, adding more milk or flour if necessary. Cover and allow to stand in a warm place for 1 hour.*
❭ *Preheat oven to 400° F.*
❭ *Form dough into 12 balls of equal size and cover. Let stand for 30 minutes.*
❭ *With a rolling pin, roll out a ball of the dough as thin as possible into a 9-inch circle. Place it in a well-buttered 9-inch pie pan and stretch the dough to reach the sides of the pan. Brush top with butter. Roll out another ball of dough and place over the first circle, and butter the top. Continue the procedure with another 4 balls of dough. Continue the same procedure with the last 6 balls of dough on a second pie plate.*
❭ *Bake for 20 minutes or until the tops become golden brown.*
❭ *While the pies are baking, mix the remaining butter with the honey.*
❭ *When the pies are done, pour half of the butter-honey mixture over the tops. Let stand for 10 minutes, then serve with the remaining butter-honey mixture on the side.*

Bulgur-Honey Dessert

Serves about 6

1 cup coarse bulgur, rinsed

½ teaspoon salt

4 cups water

1 teaspoon cinnamon

¼ teaspoon ground cloves

½ cup liquid honey

Place bulgur, salt, and water in a saucepan, then bring to boil. Cover and cook over medium-low heat for 40 minutes or until bulgur is well cooked, stirring a few times and adding more water if necessary. Stir in remaining ingredients and serve hot.

Yemeni Eggplant Salad

Serves 6 to 8

1 eggplant (about 1 pound), pierced with a fork a few times

1 small Spanish onion, finely chopped

3 tablespoons lemon juice

2 tablespoons olive oil

2 garlic cloves, crushed

1 teaspoon salt

½ teaspoon black pepper

½ teaspoon ground cumin

Fresh mint leaves

1 small firm tomato, finely chopped

This dish is often served as an appetizer, dip, or side dish.

❯ Preheat oven to 350° F.
❯ Roast eggplant for 1 hour, then remove and allow to cool. Peel eggplant, then process pulp for 1 minute in a food processor with onion, lemon juice, olive oil, garlic, salt, pepper, and cumin. Place on a flat platter, then decorate with mint leaves and tomato just before serving.

Shoubra — Meat Soup

Serves 8 to 10

2 tablespoons butter

1 pound chicken, beef, or lamb with bones, cut into pieces

4 medium potatoes, peeled and chopped

2 medium zucchini, chopped

2 medium onions, finely chopped

2 teaspoons salt

8 cups water

4 tablespoons finely chopped fresh cilantro

3 tablespoons *Zhug* (see page 155)

2 tablespoons *Hulba* (see page 156)

Arab bread (pita), toasted and broken into pieces

Melt butter in a saucepan, then sauté meat for 10 minutes. Add potatoes, zucchini, onions, salt, and water, then bring to boil. Cover and cook over medium heat for 1 hour or until meat becomes tender, adding more water if necessary. Stir in cilantro, Zhug, and Hulba. Serve immediately with toasted bread—each diner adding to taste.

Tahini-Egg Salad

Serves 4

4 tablespoons tahini

4 tablespoons lemon juice

2 garlic cloves, crushed

1 teaspoon salt

½ teaspoon black pepper

3 tablespoons water

6 hard-boiled eggs, finely chopped

4 tablespoons finely chopped fresh parsley

¼ teaspoon ground cumin

Place tahini, lemon juice, garlic, salt, pepper, and water in a blender, then blend for 1 minute. Gently mix with eggs and parsley, then spread on a platter. Sprinkle with cumin and serve.

Hor'i — Beef Shank Stew

Serves 6 to 8

3 pounds beef shanks with the bones, cut into thick slices

3 medium onions, cut into quarters

8 garlic cloves, minced

2 cups stewed tomatoes

1½ teaspoons salt

2 tablespoon *Zhug* (see page 155)

1 tablespoon *Hulba* (see page 156)

Lamb or other types of shoulder shanks can be substituted for the beef.

Place meat in a saucepan and cover with cold water to about 2 inches above the meat. Bring to boil, skimming a few times. Add the onions and garlic, then cover and reduce heat to medium-low and simmer for about 3 hours or until the meat turns tender, stirring several times and adding a little water if necessary. Stir in tomatoes and salt, then simmer uncovered over medium-low heat for 1 hour or until the juice is reduced into a somewhat thick sauce. Remove from heat, then stir in Zhug and Hulba and serve immediately.

Yemeni-Style Falafel

Makes about 4 dozen small patties

2 cups chickpeas, soaked overnight and drained

4 garlic cloves, minced

2 cups finely chopped fresh parsley

1 cup finely chopped fresh cilantro

1 cup finely chopped green onion

1 egg

2 teaspoons salt

1 teaspoon black pepper

1 teaspoon ground cumin

1 teaspoon baking soda

1 teaspoon baking powder

¼ teaspoon cayenne pepper

Oil for frying

This dish was no doubt introduced to Yemen from the Arab countries to the north, but unlike the other falafels prepared in the Middle East, often eggs are used as an ingredient in Yemen.

❯ *Place chickpeas in a food processor and process for about 1 minute. Add remaining ingredients, except oil, and process for about 4 minutes or until a dough-like paste is formed.*
❯ *Form into small patties, then deep-fry and serve warm.*

Note: *Falafel are best eaten as sandwiches by placing patties and a teaspoon each of Hulba and Zhug (see pages 156 and 155) in a bed of tomato salad in pita bread. Cut the pitas in half and make the halves into pouches.*

Salatat Banadura
Tomato Salad

Serves about 4

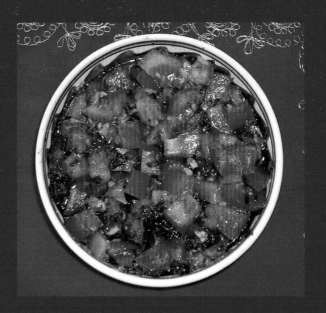

4 medium ripe but firm tomatoes, diced into ½-inch cubes

½ cup finely chopped fresh cilantro

1 garlic clove, crushed

3 tablespoons olive oil

3 tablespoons lemon juice

½ teaspoon salt

¼ teaspoon black pepper

Pinch cayenne pepper

❭ *Place tomatoes in a salad bowl and set aside.*
❭ *In a small bowl, combine remaining ingredients. Pour over tomatoes, then toss just before serving.*

Lentil Stew

Serves 8 to 10

4 tablespoons olive oil

1 pound beef or lamb, cut into small pieces

2 medium onions, finely chopped

4 tablespoons finely chopped fresh cilantro

1 cup lentils, rinsed

1½ teaspoons salt

7 cups water

2 cups stewed tomatoes

⅓ cup long-grain white rice, rinsed

4 tablespoons *Zhug* (see page 155)

2 tablespoons *Hulba* (see page 156)

A delicious filling and nutritious stew, this dish can also be prepared with more water and without rice to make a wholesome soup.

Heat oil in a saucepan, then sauté meat, onions, and cilantro over medium heat for 10 minutes. Add lentils, salt, and water and bring to boil. Cover and cook over medium heat for 1 hour. Stir in tomatoes and rice, cover, and cook for a further 25 minutes, stirring occasionally and adding more water if necessary. Stir in Zhug and Hulba, then serve hot.

CHAPTER 21

The Foods of the Greater Syria Area

A LEGACY OF A VENERABLE PAST

The culinary arts of Syria, Lebanon, Jordan, and Palestine did not develop by accident, but took shape as culture after culture flowed through the Middle East through the centuries. These histories are documented from the misty days of early civilizations until our times. Hittites, Akkadians, Assyrians, Eblans, Egyptians, Persians, Greeks, Romans, Armenians, Byzantines, Ottomans, and Europeans all left traces of their food preferences.

The cuisines of these countries reached their peak after the seventh century, during the Umayyad and Abbasid dynasties, following the establishment of the Arab Empire. In that era, with most of the known civilized world under Arab domination, great wealth flowed into the rulers' coffers and gave the impetus for development of a haute cuisine. In later centuries, Mongols, Mamluks, Ottomans, and Europeans each ruled and colonized for a while, then departed, enriching further the culinary art of the region.

In the Greater Syria area, the cosmopolitan cities of Aleppo and Damascus became the centers for the development of the culinary arts. The wealthy, with much leisure time, were able to create new dishes and adapt the old. Cooks in the palaces of the emirs vied with each other with their creations. They also wrote cookbooks, giving us glimpses into their culinary world.

Damascus, along with its sister city of Aleppo, lay at the western end of the wealth-producing Silk Road, which for some 4,000 years was the pathway of trade between the Far East and Europe. No less important in the creation of both cities' affluent lifestyle was the Frankincense Route that came overland from South Arabia carrying the silks and spices brought by Arab dhows (ships) from the Far East and Indian subcontinent, as well as the perfumes of South Arabia.

Memories of the exotic goods carried on these routes are found centuries later in the souks (marketplaces) of Damascus and Aleppo. Today, there is only one difference from the past: once carried by camel caravans, all the manufactured goods and foods found in the shops are now transported by trucks and airplanes.

Damascus and Aleppo developed a gourmet cuisine not well known in other lands. Over the centuries, other Middle Eastern cities only copied the foods of these historic urban centers. What is known today as Lebanese, Syrian, Jordanian, or Palestinian food was originally developed in the kitchens of these historic cities in their days of splendor. It is said that new dishes are not created by peasants, rather, by those with time to spare and money to experiment with new ideas.

Visitors need only enter the old quarters of Aleppo and Damascus and breathe deeply the aroma of exotic spices to feel that they are in a medieval world of action and color, a vestige from the days when these cities were unequivocally at the center of the world. The labyrinth of narrow, ancient streets; a bewildering mix of people at work or on the move; and artisans hand-pounding their brass, copper, iron, and precious metals all complement merchants offering their endless food products.

This living picture of daily activity in the medieval world is reflected in the cities' repertory of unusual recipes, many going back to the court cuisines of prior centuries. No one dining on food flavored with pomegranate syrup, grilled meat smothered in yogurt, barbecued meatballs with black cherries, or one of the dozen of varieties of kubba (ground lamb mixed with bulgur and spices) will forget the world-class cuisine of these cities.

Yet, in our times, if researchers were to survey the Arab restaurants in Europe and the Americas, they will find that the food they offer is known to the vast majority of their customers as Lebanese dishes. Even if virtually the same cuisine is found in the other countries of the Greater Syria area, the world now has come to identify it as Lebanese. The Lebanese have been so successful at marketing their food worldwide that much of its Aleppo and Damascus heritage has been forgotten. In the Arabian Gulf, countries where there are thousands of restaurants owned by people from the Greater Syria area, even the Syrians and Palestinians call the fare offered in their restaurants "Lebanese food."

No matter what the food is called or from what part of the Greater Syria area it comes, most of the dishes are healthy, nutritious, appealing, and tasty. As a child on our homestead in the western Canadian prairies, the Syrian food that I ate, such as tabbouleh and yogurt, and lentil and bulgur dishes, are now considered to be health food in North America.

Society has come a long way from when, as children in school, my siblings and I munched on our Arab food, hidden away from our peers for fear they would see us eat our sandwiches of pickled, stuffed eggplant packed in Arab bread (pita) and our 'arous bi labna (semi-solidified yogurt rolled in thin Arab bread).

Even the usual Arab condiments and sauces for these foods, some of which were beyond our means in the Depression years, are healthy, nourishing, and tasty. Garlic, lemon juice, olives, olive oil, onions, pomegranate syrup, and tahini (crushed sesame seed paste), used daily for cooking throughout most of the Arab world, are some of the healthiest food enhancers known in the culinary world. Their daily inclusion in dishes in the Greater Syria area from ancient times to ours is a testimony to their culinary attributes and healthy qualities.

These few recipes are only a small sample of gourmet cuisine offered in the Greater Syria area — today fast-spreading throughout the Western world.

Ma'muneeya — Semolina Dessert

Serves 8

4 tablespoons butter

1 cup fine semolina

1 cup whole milk

1 cup sugar

Water

1 cup whipped cream

4 tablespoons crushed pistachio nuts

This specialty pudding of Aleppo, probably one of the easiest desserts to prepare, keeps its nutritious value clandestine simply because it tastes so good.

❯ Melt butter in a saucepan over low heat, then stir-fry semolina until golden. Stir in milk and sugar, then stir over medium heat, adding a little water at a time, for 10 minutes or until the semolina is cooked into a soft paste. Place on a platter, then spread whipped cream evenly over top. Sprinkle with pistachios and serve warm.

Thoum
Damascene Garlic Appetizer

Serves about 6

1 cup mashed potatoes

6 cloves garlic, crushed

¼ cup olive oil

¼ cup plain yogurt

Salt and pepper to taste

8 black olives, pitted and sliced in half

4 medium radishes, sliced

From the earliest of time, as new products were introduced—in this case, the potato—the Damascenes took them as their own. If you like garlic, this twin of French aioli is addictive, but simpler to prepare.

Thoroughly combine potatoes, garlic, olive oil, yogurt, salt, and pepper, then place on a platter. Decorate with olives and radishes, then chill and serve.

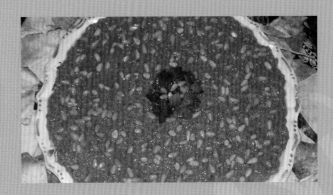

Muhammara
Roasted Red Pepper Dip

Serves 6 to 8

1½ cups ground walnuts

4 large sweet red peppers

1 tablespoon pomegranate syrup, dissolved in 2 tablespoons water

2 tablespoons lemon juice

¾ teaspoon salt

½ teaspoon ground coriander seeds

½ teaspoon ground cumin

¼ teaspoon cayenne pepper

2 tablespoons toasted pine nuts

2 tablespoons olive oil

This tasty, well-known Aleppo dish, usually served as an appetizer, adds color to the meal.

> *Preheat oven to 350° F.*
> *Place walnuts in a mixing bowl and set aside.*
> *Bake peppers on a tray for 1 hour, turning them several times, until they blister on all sides. Remove from oven and allow to cool.*
> *Skin peppers and remove seeds. Place pepper flesh in sieve for 10 minutes. Chop very finely or process in a food processor for 1 minute, then transfer to mixing bowl and combine with walnuts and remaining ingredients except pine nuts and olive oil. Spread on a platter, then chill for about 2 hours. Just before serving, decorate with pine nuts and sprinkle with olive oil. Serve with crackers or Arab bread (pita).*

Tabbouleh
Parsley and Bulgur Salad

Serves about 6 to 8

½ cup fine or medium bulgur

2 medium bunches parsley, stemmed and very finely chopped

1 cup finely chopped green onion

½ cup finely chopped fresh mint leaves

2 firm medium tomatoes, finely diced

4 tablespoons olive oil

4 tablespoons lemon juice

1 teaspoon salt

½ teaspoon black pepper

Lettuce leaves

This salad has become world-renowned. Thanks to Lebanese immigrants in the Americas and Europe, it has become a popular dish for everyone and anyone who enjoys a healthy, tasty, and light salad or side dish.

❯ *Soak bulgur in warm water for 10 minutes. Drain by pressing water out through a fine sieve. Set aside.*
❯ *In a bowl, thoroughly mix bulgur and all vegetables except lettuce leaves. Set aside.*
❯ *Combine remaining ingredients except lettuce leaves. Pour mixture over bulgur and vegetables. Toss and serve on a bed of lettuce leaves.*

Shawrbat 'Adas Ma' Ruzz
Lentil and Rice Soup

Serves about 8

4 tablespoons olive oil

2 large onions, finely chopped

4 garlic cloves, crushed

1 cup red split lentils

2 teaspoons salt

1 teaspoon black pepper

1 teaspoon ground cumin

¼ teaspoon cayenne pepper

Pinch saffron

8 cups boiling water

4 tablespoons long-grain white rice, rinsed

2 tablespoons very finely chopped fresh cilantro

2 tablespoons lemon juice

A popular soup in the Greater Syria region, it can be served as is or pureed. Its crowning glory is when fresh cilantro and lemon juice are added. It is a great meal on its own for cold winter evenings.

Heat oil over medium in a saucepan, then sauté onions until they begin to brown. Add garlic and stir-fry for a further 3 minutes. Add the remaining ingredients except cilantro and lemon juice. Bring to boil, then cover and cook over medium heat for 40 minutes or until lentils are tender, adding more water if necessary. Remove from heat, then stir in cilantro and lemon juice and serve.

Harraqa Usba'u — Lentil Dumplings

Serves 8 to 10

1 cup lentils, rinsed

7 cups water

½ pound bread dough

Salt and pepper to taste

½ teaspoon ground cumin

⅛ teaspoon cayenne pepper

3 tablespoons lemon juice

4 tablespoons olive oil

1 large onion, finely chopped

Cooking oil

½ cup finely chopped fresh cilantro

4 garlic cloves, crushed

Seeds of 1 pomegranate

A dish unique to Damascus, *Harraqa Usba'u* is one of the most traditional and famous dishes of the city.

> *Place lentils and water in a saucepan and bring to boil. Cover and cook over medium heat for 30 minutes.*
> *In the meantime, roll dough until about ⅛ inch thick, then cut into ½-inch squares. Add half of the squares, salt, pepper, cumin, and cayenne pepper to the lentils, then cook for a further 15 minutes or until the dough is cooked. Add lemon juice and stir. Set aside, but keep hot.*
> *Heat olive oil over medium in a frying pan, then sauté onion until light brown. Stir the frying pan contents into lentils.*
> *In the same frying pan, add cooking oil to 1 inch deep or enough to deep-fry remainder of dough squares until they turn light brown. Remove with a slotted spoon. Place in a serving dish and set aside.*
> *Combine cilantro and garlic. Place in another serving dish and set aside.*
> *Serve lentils in soup bowls. Each diner may add fried bread, cilantro, garlic, and pomegranate seeds to taste.*

Fattat Hummus
Chickpea and Yogurt Platter

Serves 6

2 medium loaves Arab bread (pita), toasted
and broken into small pieces
1 (19-ounce) can chickpeas, drained
1 cup plain yogurt
1 clove garlic, crushed
1 teaspoon salt
½ teaspoon black pepper
Seeds of 1 pomegranate
2 tablespoons lemon juice
1 tablespoon tahini
2 tablespoons butter
4 tablespoons pine nuts or slivered almonds
2 tablespoons chopped fresh parsley

In Damascus, this dish is usually served
as a part of a hearty breakfast.

❯ Spread bread pieces evenly on a platter, then
spread chickpeas evenly over top and set aside.
❯ Thoroughly combine yogurt, garlic, salt, pepper,
pomegranate seeds, lemon juice, and tahini,
then spread over chickpeas.
❯ Melt butter in a frying pan, then sauté pine nuts
or almonds until they begin to brown. Spread
nuts over yogurt mixture, decorate with
parsley, and serve.

Kafta bil Karaz
Barbecued Meatballs with Cherries

Serves about 4

1 pound finely ground lean lamb
¾ teaspoon salt
½ teaspoon black pepper
½ teaspoon allspice
½ teaspoon ground cumin
½ teaspoon ground coriander seeds
¼ teaspoon cinnamon
¼ teaspoon nutmeg
⅛ teaspoon cayenne pepper
Large fresh cherries (or canned or candied),
pitted (1 cherry per meatball)

In Aleppo, a special kind of bitter black cherry,
only found around the city, is used when
preparing this dish.

In a food processor, process for 1 minute all
ingredients except cherries. Form into small
balls about 1 inch in diameter, wetting hands
to keep meat from sticking. On skewers, slide
one ball then one cherry for a total of 4 of each
per skewer. Gently press the balls by hand to
elongate. Barbecue until meat is done—from
5 to 10 minutes. Serve hot with cooked rice.

Kafta Mabrouma — Ground Meat with Pine Nuts

Serves 6 to 8

2 medium onions, very finely chopped

4 garlic cloves, crushed

1 egg, beaten

2 pounds finely ground lean lamb

2 teaspoons salt

1 teaspoon black pepper

½ teaspoon allspice

¼ teaspoon Aleppo pepper (see "Asian Condiments" section)

4 tablespoons pine nuts

4 tablespoons melted butter

4 tablespoons water

2 tablespoons coarsely chopped fresh parsley

1 lemon, sliced

This is a specialty of Aleppo, where it is baked and served in a round platter with the rolls arranged in diminishing circles.

❯ *Preheat oven to 350° F.*

❯ *In a mixing bowl, thoroughly combine onions, garlic, egg, meat, salt, pepper, allspice, and Aleppo pepper. Flatten mixture until about ¼ inch thick, then cut into 6 rectangular pieces. Press pine nuts along the longer side edge of each rectangle, then roll into a sausage shape. Slightly bend to fit into a round baking dish. Place first* **kafta** *roll along inside edge of dish, then continue with the remaining 5 rolls, fitting them tightly together. Brush with butter and sprinkle with water. Cover and bake for 1 hour or until rolls are well cooked, baking uncovered for the last 20 minutes. Place on a hot serving platter, then garnish with parsley and lemon slices. Serve with cooked rice or fried potatoes.*

CHAPTER 22

Turkish Food

ONE OF THE THREE GREAT CUISINES IN THE WORLD

Visitors unfamiliar with Turkish food are usually surprised when they first taste it. And well they should, for Turkish food has a long and distinguished history. It has been accorded the status as one of the three great cuisines of the world, along with the Chinese and the French. Generally speaking, most basic cuisines rely on one simple element. For example, pasta forms the essence of Italian food, while French cuisine is based on sauces. Turkish cuisine, however, features many types of foods and an infinite variety of preparation methods.

The grand and imperial kitchens of the world resulted from a nurturing environment that ultimately produced an abundance of foodstuffs, a long social tradition, and an imperial culinary legacy—all elements possessed by the Turks. The large Ottoman Empire that included the whole Middle East, most of North Africa, and all of the Balkan nations, came into contact with many cultures and their foods. In addition, Turkey's strategic location between Europe and the Middle East influenced the foods of the Ottomans, and, in turn, Ottoman cuisine had an impact on the cuisines of the others.

The origin of the Turkish kitchen can be traced back to Central Asia, the original homeland of the Turks. In the ensuing centuries, during their slow migration westward to Asia Minor, they encountered a great number of culinary tastes, which they took on as their own. This culminated in the Ottoman Imperial kitchen, formed during the 600 years of that dynasty's reign.

When they were herdsmen in Central Asia,

the Turks were great consumers of meat, milk, and other dairy products. Milk and cream were the usual breakfast food, as well as milk that was dried and stored as a powder for future use. Above all, yogurt, which the Turks claim as their own contribution to the world, was the basic dairy product in the diet of the people.

Equally important were the meat dishes that were mainly grilled, roasted in underground ovens, or cooked and preserved in their own fat for later use, all still part of Turkish cooking methods for meat. However, in their westward odyssey, the Turks picked up new ingredients to add to their meat dishes, such as fruits, vegetables, and spices, and perfected the process using meat to stuff vegetables. In the march of history, many other influences crept into the food of the huge Ottoman Empire. The old civilizations of the Middle East—Arab, Persian, and Byzantine—all had a part in the creation of the Turkish kitchen. The kebab is of Arab origin; pilav (pilaf) is the Turkish version of the Persian pulau; while the Turkish inheritance from the Byzantines is manifested in the Greek names for a number of fish and seafood dishes.

In the medieval centuries, the meeting of the Arab, Greek, Persian, and Turkish elements was largely instrumental in producing the Ottoman Imperial kitchen—a huge establishment that, in the year 1723, counted 1,370 kitchen staff and used 30,000 head of cattle, 160,000 sheep, and 100,000 pigeons to prepare the required meals for the palace personnel. In Topkapi, the sultan's palace in Istanbul, chefs refined their dishes, and eventually these gastronomic delights were filtered down to the peoples' kitchens, a rich legacy reflected in the Turkish food of our day.

The beauty of the Turkish cuisine is that it is mainly based on fresh ingredients and simple cooking methods. Dishes are presented simply, not hidden under sauces or complicated presentations. It is said that the Turks prepare eggplant over forty ways, and each of these dishes is quite simple to make.

Besides pulses (edible seeds) such as chickpeas and lentils, bulgur, a cooked, then dried and crushed wheat, is very important in the Turkish diet. Rice and a homemade noodle the Turks inherited from the Chinese are also often part of everyday meals. Fresh fruits and vegetables, grown in abundance, are consumed in great quantities, fresh in season and dried in winter. As for fats, olive oil has, through the centuries, largely replaced the butter formerly used by nomadic Turks.

Fish and meat kebabs, delicately spiced depending on the region, are world-renowned. Delicious casseroles cooked in earthenware, as well as moist and tender vegetable- and meat-based stews—the staples of lunchtime cafeterias—are delicious and nourishing.

The most commonly used seasonings and condiments are cinnamon, cumin, coriander seed, dill, garlic, mint, mustard, onions, and parsley, as well as the sour spice sumac. Yogurt and Aleppo pepper, a semi-hot capsicum, are often served as side condiments. Grape syrup and all kinds of nuts, especially almonds, hazelnuts, and pistachios, are considered essential when preparing desserts. In homes and some restaurants, the meals often end with a beautifully presented selection of seasonal fruits, such as green almonds, apples, pears, plums, pomegranates, and strawberries. At other times, traditional Turkish sweets such as lokum, baklava, kadayif, halva, or rice pudding conclude the meal with a heavenly sweet touch, especially when enhanced by steaming demitasses of Turkish coffee.

When visiting Turkey, one should sip ayran, a yogurt drink, on a hot summer day; sit down to a breakfast of freshly baked bread, along with olives, cheese, fresh vegetables, boiled eggs, creamy yogurt, and honey; enjoy a lunch of lentil soup, bulgur or rice pilaf, and chicken baked with peppers and eggplant; and at the last meal of the day, nibble on numerous mazza dishes, then dine on tasty kebabs and cap the meal with one of Turkey's renowned sweets. It can then be said that one has tasted a bit of the Turkish Imperial cuisine.

Of course, these few recipes will only open the door slightly to the culinary world of the sultans and only give one a small taste of its pleasures.

Ayran — Yogurt Drink

Makes about 8 drinks

4 cups yogurt
2 cups water
1 cup half-and-half
1 teaspoon salt
Crushed ice
Fresh mint leaves, finely chopped

In a blender, blend all ingredients, except crushed ice and mint leaves, for 1 minute. Serve with crushed ice and garnish with mint leaves, or refrigerate for later use.

Ezo Gelin – Lentil Soup

Serves about 8

1 cup split red lentils
9 cups water
2 onions, finely chopped
½ cup long-grain white rice, rinsed
4 garlic cloves, crushed
2 tablespoons tomato paste
2 tablespoons lemon juice
2 teaspoons salt
1 teaspoon black pepper
1 teaspoon ground cumin
⅛ teaspoon cayenne pepper
4 tablespoons butter
2 tablespoons dried mint

> *Place lentils, water, onions, and rice in a saucepan, then bring to boil and cover. Cook over medium-low heat for 40 minutes, stirring a few times. Stir in garlic, tomato paste, lemon juice, salt, pepper, cumin, and cayenne pepper, then cook for 5 minutes.*
> *In the meantime, melt butter in a frying pan, then stir in mint and remove from heat.*
> *Place soup in a serving bowl, then stir in frying pan contents and serve.*

Mas Piyazi
Mung Bean Salad

Serves 6 to 8

1 cup dried mung beans, rinsed
1 cup finely chopped green onion
2 garlic cloves, crushed
½ cup finely chopped fresh cilantro
1 teaspoon paprika
1 teaspoon salt
⅛ teaspoon cayenne pepper
3 tablespoons olive oil
4 tablespoons lemon juice
2 tablespoons pomegranate seeds

Place beans in a saucepan and cover with cold water to about 2 inches above the beans, then bring to boil. Cover saucepan, then cook over medium-low heat for about 40 minutes or until mung beans are tender. Drain beans and allow to cool, then place in a salad bowl. Stir in remaining ingredients except pomegranate seeds. Sprinkle pomegranate seeds on top, then serve.

Mucver – Zucchini Patties

Makes 20 to 24 patties

2 cups grated zucchini
1 cup finely chopped fresh parsley
½ cup finely chopped onion
½ cup finely chopped and seeded sweet pepper
½ cup crumbled feta cheese
½ cup white flour
1 teaspoon salt
½ teaspoon black pepper
4 eggs, beaten
Oil for frying

> Combine all ingredients, except eggs and oil, then stir in eggs and set aside.

> Place oil in saucepan to about 1 inch deep, then heat over medium. Deep fry over medium heat by dropping tablespoons of batter in oil, turning over once until golden. Drain on paper towels, then serve hot or cold.

Izgara Bulgurlu Kofte
Meat and Bulgur Patties

Serves about 6

½ cup fine bulgur
1 pound ground lamb or beef
1 large onion, chopped
1 large sweet pepper, seeded and chopped
1 cup mashed potatoes
2 garlic cloves, crushed
¼ cup fine bread crumbs
½ cup finely chopped fresh parsley
4 tablespoons finely chopped fresh cilantro
2½ teaspoons salt
1 teaspoon black pepper
1 teaspoon ground cumin
1 teaspoon dried oregano
⅛ teaspoon cayenne pepper

> Soak bulgur in warm water for 10 minutes. Squeeze out water by pressing it through a fine sieve.

> Preheat oven to 350° F.

> Place all ingredients in a food processor, then blend until consistency of bread dough, adding more bread crumbs if necessary. Roll dough into walnut-size balls and flatten into patties, then place in a greased baking pan. Bake, uncovered, for 45 minutes or until done.

Basbousa bil Loz
Almond Pudding

Serves 8

1 cup sugar

1½ cups water

1 tablespoon lemon juice

½ teaspoon almond extract

6 tablespoons butter

½ cup finely ground almonds

½ cup fine semolina

Whipped cream

❯ *In a saucepan, boil sugar and water, stirring a few times. Stir in lemon juice and almond extract, then simmer for a few minutes. Set syrup aside, but keep warm.*

❯ *Melt butter in a frying pan, then stir-fry almonds and semolina over low heat until they begin to turn light brown. Slowly add syrup to almonds and semolina while stirring constantly. Continue until puddings thickens, then remove from heat.*

❯ *Pour into pudding cups, then decorate with whipped cream and serve warm.*

Hunkar Begendi
Eggplant Puree

Serves 4 to 6

1 eggplant (about 1 pound)

2 tablespoons lemon juice

2 tablespoons butter

2 tablespoons white flour

¼ cup hot milk

½ teaspoon salt

½ teaspoon black pepper

⅛ teaspoon nutmeg

2 tablespoons Parmesan cheese

2 tablespoons finely chopped fresh cilantro

❯ *Preheat oven to 350° F.*

❯ *Take a fork and pierce the eggplant a few times all around.*

❯ *Bake eggplant in oven for 1 hour or until well baked. Allow to cool, then remove skin. Mash pulp, then simmer over medium-low heat for 10 minutes in a saucepan with lemon juice, stirring frequently.*

❯ *In the meantime, place butter and flour in a frying pan, then, stirring constantly, cook over medium heat until flour turns light brown. Stir frying pan contents, milk, salt, pepper, and nutmeg into eggplant. Keep stirring until mixture takes on the consistency of mashed potatoes, adding more milk if necessary. Stir in cheese, then cook over low heat for 1 minute. Spread on a platter, then decorate with cilantro and serve warm.*

Lokoum – Turkish Delight

1 cup sugar

½ cup water

1 lemon rind, grated

2 tablespoons gelatin, dissolved in ½ cup warm water

1 teaspoon rose water

1 teaspoon almond extract

4 tablespoons orange juice

4 tablespoons coarsely ground pistachios

4 tablespoons coarsely ground almonds

Powdered sugar

Even though not truly authentic, this is a fast and easy way to make Turkish delight.

Boil sugar, water, and lemon rind in a saucepan. Stir in gelatin, rose water, and almond extract. Cover and simmer over low heat for 12 minutes, then stir in orange juice, pistachios, and almonds. Pour into a greased 8-inch square pan and refrigerate overnight. Cut into 1-inch squares, then dunk into powdered sugar and serve. Store in a cool place.

Harput Koftesi
Bulgur Meatballs

Serves 6 to 8

1 cup fine bulgur

1 pound ground beef or lamb

1 large onion, very finely chopped

½ teaspoon allspice

2 teaspoons salt

1 teaspoon paprika

½ teaspoon black pepper

½ teaspoon cumin

¼ teaspoon cayenne pepper

3 tablespoons butter

2 large tomatoes, finely chopped

4 cups water

❯ *Soak bulgur in warm water for 10 minutes. Squeeze out water by pressing it through a fine sieve.*
❯ *Thoroughly combine bulgur, beef, onion, allspice, 1½ teaspoons of the salt, ½ teaspoon of the paprika, ¼ teaspoon of both the pepper and cumin, and ⅛ teaspoon of cayenne pepper. Shape into balls a little smaller than a walnut and set aside.*
❯ *Melt butter in a saucepan, then add tomatoes and the remaining salt, paprika, pepper, cumin, and cayenne pepper. Fry over medium heat for 8 minutes, then add water and bring to boil. Add balls, then cover and cook over medium-low heat for 45 minutes or until balls are well done.*

References

Algar, Ayla. *Classical Turkish Cooking. Harper Collins Publisher: New York, 2001.*

Anderson, Eugene N. The Food of China. *Yale University Press: New Haven, 1988.*

Balasuriya, Heather J. and Winegar, Karin. Fire and Spice: The Cuisine of Sri Lanka. *McGraw Hill Pub: New York, 1989.*

Basan, Ghillie. Classic Turkish Cooking. *St. Martin's Press: New York, 1997.*

Batra, Neelam. 1000 Indian Recipes. *Wiley Pub. Inc: New York, 2002.*

Benghiat, Suzy. Middle Eastern Cooking. *Smithbooks: Toronto, 1984.*

Brissenden, Rosemary. South East Asian Food, *Hardie Grant Books: Australia, 2003.*

Bullis, Douglas and Hutton, Wendy. The Food of Sri Lanka. *Periplus Editions (HK) Ltd: Singapore, 2001.*

Chandra, Smita and Sanjeev. Cuisines of India. *The Ecco Press, Imprint of HarperCollins Publishers Inc: New York, 2001.*

Cheboro, Lina B. and Halawani, Nada M. Arabic Cooking: Step by Step. *Arab Scientific Publishers: Beirut, 1997.*

Corey, Helen. The Art of Syrian Cookery. *Doubleday & Company Inc: New York, 1962.*

Dassanayaka,Channa. Sri Lankan Flavours. *Hardie Grant Books: Australia, 2003.*

Day, Harvey. Encyclopaedia of Natural Health and Healing. *Woodbridge Press Publishing Company: Santa Barbara, 1979.*

Deh-Ta Hsiung. The Chinese Kitchen. *Kyle Cathie Ltd: London, 1999.*

Deh-Ta Hsiung and Simonds, Nina. The Food of China. *Murdoch Books: Australia, 2001.*

Dunlop, Fuchsia. Land of Plenty: A Treasury of Authentic Sichuan Cooking. *W.W. Norton & Co: New York, 2003.*

Gress, Priti C. Flavorful India. *Hippocrene Books: New York, 2005.*

Harris, L. John. The Book of Garlic. *Arris Books: Berkeley, 1975.*

Hendrickson, Robert. Lewd Food: The Complete Guide to Aphrodisiac Edibles. *Chilton Book Co: Radnor, PA, 1974.*

Hepinstall, Hi Soo Shin. Growing Up in a Korean Kitchen. *Ten Speed Press: Toronto, 2001.*

Jaffrey, Madhur. An Invitation to Indian Cooking. *Alfred A. Knopf: New York, 1973.*

——. Illustrated Indian Cookery. *BBC Books: London, 1982.*

——. From Curries to Kebabs. *Clarkson Potter Pub: New York, 2005.*

Kwak, Jenny, Dok Suni. Recipes from My Mother's Korean Kitchen. *St. Martin's Press: New York, 1998.*

Laing, Lucille. Chinese Regional Cooking. *Sterling Pub. Co.*

Inc: New York, 1979.*

Law, Ruth. The Southeast Asia Cookbook. *D.I. Fine: New York, 1990.*

Mallos, Tess. The Complete Middle Eastern Cookbook. *McGraw-Hill Book Co: Toronto, 1979.*

Marks, Copeland. The Varied Kitchens of India. *M. Evans & Co. Inc: New York, 1986.*

——. The Exotic Kitchens of Indonesia, *M. Evans & Co. Inc: New York, 1993.*

Nasrallah, Nawal. Delights from the Garden of Eden. *1st Books: Bloomington, IN, 2004.*

Nguyen, Andrea Q. Into the Vietnamese Kitchen. *Ten Speed Press: Berkeley, 2006.*

Oseland, James. Cradle of Flavor. *W. W. Norton & Co Inc: New York, 2006.*

Roden, Claudia. Middle Eastern Food. *Penguin Books Ltd: Middlesex, England, 1970.*

Salloum, Habeeb. From the Lands of Figs and Olives: Over 300 Delicious and Unusual Recipes from the Middle East and North Africa. *Interlink Books: New York, 1995.*

——. Classic Vegetarian Cooking from the Middle East and North Africa. *Interlink Books: New York, 2000.*

——. Arab Cooking on a Saskatchewan Homestead: Recipes and Recollections. *Canadian Plains Research Center, University of Regina: Regina, Canada, 2005.*

Shaida, Margaret. The Legendary Cuisine of Persia. *Interlink Books: New York, 2002.*

Simonds, Nina. Classic Chinese Cuisine. *Chapters Pub. Ltd: Vermont, 1994.*

Takahashi, Kuwako. The Joy of Japanese Cooking. *Tuttle Pub: Singapore, 2002.*

Thompson, David. Thai Food. *Ten Speed Press: Berkeley, 2002.*

Trang, Corinne. Essentials of Asian Cuisine. *Simon & Schuster: New York, 2003.*

Tsuji, Shizuo. Japanese Cooking: A Simple Art. *Kodansha International: Tokyo, 1980.*

Westrip, Joyce. Moghul Cooking: India's Courtly Cuisine. *Serif: London, 1997.*

Woodward, Sarah. The Ottoman Kitchen. *Interlink Books: New York, 2001.*

Wright, Clifford A. A Mediterranean Feast. *William Morrow and Company, Inc: New York, 1999.*

Yan-Kit, So. Classic Food of China. *Macmillan: London, 1992.*

Yassine, Sima Osman and Kamal, Sadouf. Middle Eastern Cuisine. *Dar El-Ilm-Malayin: Beirut, 1984.*

Zayani, Afnan R. A Taste of the Arabian Gulf. *Ministry of Information: Bahrain, 1988.*